ACTIVELY CARING FOR PEOPLE **IN SCHOOLS**

ACTIVELY CARING
FOR PEOPLE
IN SCHOOLS

*How to Cultivate
a Culture of*
COMPASSION

E. SCOTT GELLER, PhD

NEW YORK

NASHVILLE MELBOURNE

ACTIVELY CARING FOR PEOPLE IN SCHOOLS
How to Cultivate a Culture of COMPASSION

Published in New York, New York, by Morgan James Publishing. Morgan James and The Entrepreneurial Publisher are trademarks of Morgan James, LLC.
www.MorganJamesPublishing.com

The Morgan James Speakers Group can bring authors to your live event. For more information or to book an event visit The Morgan James Speakers Group at www.TheMorganJamesSpeakersGroup.com.

Shelfie

A **free** eBook edition is available
with the purchase of this print book.

CLEARLY PRINT YOUR NAME ABOVE IN UPPER CASE

Instructions to claim your free eBook edition:
1. Download the Shelfie app for Android or iOS
2. Write your name in **UPPER CASE** above
3. Use the Shelfie app to submit a photo
4. Download your eBook to any device

ISBN 978-1-68350-249-4 paperback
ISBN 978-1-68350-250-0 eBook
Library of Congress Control Number:
2016915545

Cover Design by:
Rachel Lopez
www.r2cdesign.com

Interior Design by:
Bonnie Bushman
The Whole Caboodle Graphic Design

In an effort to support local communities, raise awareness and funds, Morgan James Publishing donates a percentage of all book sales for the life of each book to Habitat for Humanity Peninsula and Greater Williamsburg.

Get involved today! Visit
www.MorganJamesBuilds.com

TABLE OF CONTENTS

FOREWORD BY BOBBY KIPPER

The phone rang and as I looked down I noticed that my daughter, Jolie, who I had dropped off at Virginia Tech as a new student a month earlier was calling. "Dad, you need to meet my Psychology Professor, Dr. Geller," was her statement. Jolie had listened to Dr. E. Scott Geller's lectures in her introductory psychology class, and realized her renowned professor and I had a great deal in common. She believed we were both on the same page regarding our attempts to make the world a kinder and more compassionate place. Jolie had connected the dots of two men who believe in the true dignity of human rights.

So I reached out to Scott Geller in an effort to just say hello and let him know how much my daughter respected him. What I found was a true ambassador for humankind who became an instant friend and partner to make a positive impact on our society. Scott Geller epitomizes the notion that one person can truly make a difference.

Dr. Geller is more than a distinguished alumni professor of over forty-five years at Virginia Tech. He is a society change agent. As the father of Actively Caring for People (AC4P), he has given the world new life to building and nourishing communities of interpersonal compassion and kindness.

As the Executive Director of the National Center for the Prevention of Community Violence (NCPVP), I saw AC4P as a significant process in our mission to prevent and reduce violence. We are honored that Professor Geller has partnered with our Center to take the AC4P process to America's policing operations throughout communities. In that regard, we have recently co-authored a teaching/learning manual that is now serving as a cornerstone for building positive police/citizen relations in America. In the first year alone, this policing process has already been introduced to nearly 30 communities across the U.S.

While we are extremely proud of this effort, a change agent's work is never done. The vision of the AC4P Movement is greater than community police departments. Now our vision is to move into the world of community schools. What parent would not want their child to attend a school that has the reputation of students and staff actively caring for one another? Through the AC4P Movement for schools, this is now a reality.

But this book is more than an ivory-tower idea. It's about a life-improving process at a time ripe for implementation. A time when bullies become friends, when staff and students embrace a new level of mutual respect, and when school climate is driven by interpersonal compassion and actively caring. If this is the school you want for your family and community, look no further. It's all right here in the pages that follow. It warms my heart to know that not only has one man made a beneficial difference; he continues to make that difference.

Bobby Kipper, Director
National Center for the Prevention of Community Violence
bobbykipper@solveviolence.com

THE INITIATION AND EVOLUTION
OF THE AC4P MOVEMENT

I coined the term "actively caring" in 1990 while working with a team of safety leaders at Exxon Chemical in Baytown, Texas. Our vision was to create and sustain a brother/sister keeper's culture in which everyone looks out for each other's safety every day. This requires people to routinely go above and beyond the call of duty on behalf of the health, safety, and well-being of others. The team agreed "actively caring for people" (AC4P) was an ideal label for this company-wide paradigm shift. Most people do care about the well-being of others, but few "act" on their caring nature. The challenge: to get everyone to *actively care.*

Following the Virginia Tech tragedy on April 16, 2007, when an armed student took the lives of 32 students and faculty and injured 17 others, the AC4P concept assumed a new focus and prominence for my students and me. In a time of great uncertainty and reflection on campus, those most affected by the tragedy did not think about themselves, but acted to help classmates, friends, and even strangers heal. This collective effort was manifested in an AC4P Movement for culture change (see www.ac4p.org), making the belongingness spirit of the Virginia Tech Hokie community even stronger. My students and I envisioned spreading this AC4P Movement beyond VT using a basic principle of behavioral science—positive reinforcement.

We took the green silicon wristbands engraved with "Actively Caring for People" that I had distributed at safety conferences for almost two decades and added a numbering system. This enabled computer tracking of the AC4P process: *See*, *Act*, *Pass*, and *Share* (SAPS). The SAPS process asks individuals and groups to look for AC4P behavior (i.e., See) and reward such AC4P behavior with a green wristband (i.e., Act).

Wristband recipients are then requested to look for AC4P behavior from others and pass on the wristband (i.e., Pass). They are asked to document this exchange (including the nature of the AC4P behavior) at the AC4P website (www.ac4p.org), along with the wristband number. In this way, a recognition process is tracked worldwide (i.e., **S**hare) as positive AC4P communication.

THE U.S. EDUCATIONAL SYSTEM

The current educational paradigm in U.S. schools, supported by school resource officers (SROs), is more about "the blame game" and finding fault for mistakes rather than focusing on successes. Standardized test outcomes take precedence over learning processes; disincentives and penalties trump positive consequences for a host of behaviors. How teachers teach, students learn, administrators lead, and parents interact with their children and school personnel are all negatively affected. We need flourishing positive relationships, a "we" over "me" mindset, and AC4P behavior as a societal norm.

Educators, SROs, students, parents, and community members can *empower* each other to use the AC4P principles and applications revealed in this teaching guide. Together, we can enhance students' self-esteem, self-efficacy, personal control, optimism, and sense of belonging. The end result: a culture of interpersonal compassion throughout all grade levels at our schools.

THE AC4P AND BULLYING PREVENTION

Targeted criteria for selecting a bullying-prevention program are provided by Colvin, Tobin, Beard, Hagan, and Sprague.[1] Specifically, they advise the intervention to be: 1) supported by research; 2) based on behavioral science; and 3) emphasize the teaching of prosocial behavior to replace bullying behavior.

But many American schools attempt to curb bullying by turning to rule enforcement and punishment. School psychologists have reported the three most frequently used intervention strategies: 1) discussions between school personnel and bullies after bullying incidents; 2) negative consequences (e.g., suspension) for bullying; and 3) heightened supervision in less structured places (e.g., the playground). [1]

Classroom rules, teacher training, and improved classroom management were identified in a meta-analysis as the most frequently-used program elements.[2] Unfortunately, traditional anti-bullying interventions have a poor history of effectiveness.[3] Additionally, punitive approaches to behavior change have a number of serious short- and long-term disadvantages.[4] A distinctly different and positive approach is needed to prevent bullying.

The behavioral science components of AC4P intervention detailed in this manual focus on: a) improving observable behavior; b) using activators to direct behavior; and c) applying positive consequences to motivate behavior.

AC4P interventions also use: a) supportive feedback and recognition as positive consequences to reward AC4P behavior, increase perceived competence and fuel self-motivation; b) evidence-based strategies to enhance perceived empowerment and self-motivation; and c) interpersonal communication to boost self-esteem, self-efficacy, personal control, optimism, belongingness, and interdependence.

TANGIBLE AND SOCIAL REWARDS

Students who bully seek power and coercive dominance, find satisfaction in causing harm and suffering to other students, and are often recognized for their aggressive behavior with tangible or social rewards.[5] Given the responsiveness of these students to rewards, an anti-bullying intervention should include an incentive/reward contingency that promotes behavior contrary to bullying.

In fact, a widely-practiced and effective way to eliminate an undesirable behavior is to reward desirable behavior incompatible with the undesirable behavior.[6] This translates to rewarding prosocial behavior in lieu of bully-related behavior.

Any action that benefits another person is prosocial behavior.[7] It includes sharing, helping, cooperating, donating, and volunteering. Research suggests a school-based approach that focuses on modeling prosocial behavior has potential as an anti-bullying intervention.

For example, Honig and Pollack demonstrated that one month of daily discussions with second graders sharing their prosocial actions between themselves and others, increased the number of prosocial actions observed among students, compared to classrooms without these daily discussion sessions.[8] In fact, Demaray and Malecki specifically recommended social support as a program-enhancing component for bullying prevention.[9]

BEHAVIORAL EXPECTATIONS

Setting clear behavioral norms by "developing classroom and school-wide rules that prohibit bullying, as well as adult modeling of respectful and nonviolent behavior" is suggested by Whitted and Dupper.[10] School-wide and classroom policies are frequently established to set behavioral expectations in schools.[3]

But to eliminate a specific behavior (e.g., bullying behavior), it's more effective to set success-seeking objectives (i.e., goals with positive consequences) rather than failure-avoiding policies.[11] The AC4P approach to bullying prevention introduces prosocial/AC4P behaviors as expectations to facilitate a new social norm of interpersonal AC4P behavior among peers.

Students are strongly influenced by their peer group. Students are more likely to become prosocial when they have prosocial classmates.[12] Fewer problems among first graders from unstable homes were found if they were in classrooms with a relatively high frequency of prosocial behavior, according to Hoglund and Leadbeater.[13] Given the benefits of a prosocial approach, we expect less bullying when an intervention increases the frequency of prosocial behaviors.

ENHANCING SOCIAL COMPETENCE

Interactive teaching techniques are recommended by Whitted and Dupper to enhance social competence.[10] Social competence is one's assessment of his or her ability to interact effectively with peers.[14] Most students could potentially benefit from prosocial interactions aimed at enhancing social competence. Individuals lacking social competence are more likely to be victims of bullying and to bully others.[15]

But students are rarely provided with opportunities to develop their social skills within existing bullying-prevention programs. School psychologists have indicated that top-down approaches, such as classroom rules against bullying, are implemented frequently (89.6%), compared to alternative bullying-reduction strategies that can foster social competence, such as student-peer counseling for victims (26.4%), student-led anti-bullying activities (34.9%), and formal participation of students in decision-making about bullying (36.3%).[1]

Our AC4P approach aims to involve all students, beyond bullies and victims, and provide opportunities for everyone to model and recognize AC4P behaviors performed by classmates. Our first bullying-prevention intervention was consistent with the AC4P principles detailed in this guidebook, and we introduced it as an "Actively Caring for People" process. This AC4P intervention activated modeling and rewarded desired AC4P behavior.

The AC4P approach was based on humanism and applied behavioral science (ABS)—*humanistic behaviorism*. Tangible rewards and social approval promote prosocial behaviors incompatible with bullying, aligning with the intervention guidelines recommended by Colvin etal.[1] and Whitted and Dupper.[10]

AC4P INTERVENTION PLAN

To increase prosocial behavior, our intervention program established an "if-then" contingency to motivate AC4P behavior among fourth, fifth, and sixth-grade students. To be eligible to wear a green wristband engraved with the message, "Actively Caring for People," students wrote a story about a specific AC4P behavior they observed, or they performed an AC4P behavior themselves and had it documented in a story written by another student.

At the start of each day, the classroom teacher selected three AC4P stories to read aloud to the class, publically recognizing the students in each story. From these three stories, one was selected and the pair of students involved— the good-deed performer and the observer—were each given a green AC4P wristband. These two students wore the AC4P wristband for the entire day, as the "Actively-Caring Heroes of the Day." This cycle of sharing AC4P stories and recognizing certain AC4P observers and performers was repeated each day for five consecutive weeks.

The teacher's selection of stories to read each day and the one story to use for the wristband reward was not random. During the five-week intervention, every student was given an opportunity to be recognized at least once as the AC4P observer and once as the AC4P performer. To increase the likelihood the class would meet the team goal of every student participating at least once as both an observer and a performer, we suggested teachers pick stories from students who rarely submit them.

Each week from Weeks 2 to 6, the teacher facilitated relationship-building and belongingness among classmates by randomly pairing students for interpersonal discussions. At these weekly sessions, students discussed one of the following statements or questions: a) What do you want to be when you grow up?; b) Share a secret talent you have or something you do really well; c) What is your greatest fear, and why?; d) What do you like most about school, and why?; and e) Share something new about yourself.

The purpose of this exchange was to foster new relationships among the students and potentially make interpersonal AC4P behavior easier to perform and observe throughout the five-week intervention phase. Students were told everyone would receive their own AC4P wristband to keep at the end of program if everyone contributed at least one AC4P story and was observed performing at least one AC4P behavior.

EVALUATION PLAN

An ABS time-series design was implemented, consisting of a Baseline phase during Week 1, an Intervention phase during Weeks 2 to 6, and a Withdrawal phase at Week 7.

Every Friday, students completed the same survey that addressed both the AC4P and bully-related behaviors observed, received, and performed. Other survey questions assessed personal perceptions and attitudes toward AC4P. Students anonymously completed the surveys and had the choice to answer all, some, or none of the questions. Informed consent was implied by the return of a survey.

RESULTS

The details of this AC4P intervention to prevent bullying behavior at two elementary schools and the remarkable results are presented elsewhere in professional research journals.[16]

Here I give you only a brief overview to demonstrate the extremely positive impact of our first AC4P approach to decrease the frequency of interpersonal bullying behavior, and increase students' self-esteem and interpersonal sharing.

After the intervention weeks, every student in all eight classrooms at one elementary school (n=199 students) and in 16 classrooms at a second elementary school (n=404 students) submitted at least one AC4P story and performed a minimum of one AC4P behavior, achieving the classroom goal needed for all students to receive and keep an AC4P wristband. For both schools, the frequencies of observed bulling behavior, bulling of others, and victimization due to bulling decreased more than 50%.

Each week, a majority of students in the classrooms did not receive the wristband reward, because a maximum of only ten students could be recognized weekly. Yet, marked increases in self-esteem occurred every week for each grade. A concomitant increase in an estimate of self-esteem was a positive side-effect of the significant weekly decline in bullying for all grades.

At the conclusion of the AC4P intervention in the second elementary school referred to above, the Principal requested to use the phrase "Actively Caring for People" on a stained glass window.

The photograph depicts the special stained-glass window displayed prominently in the school cafeteria. The sixth-grade students voted for this window as their class gift to the school.

Bottom line: A prosocial incentive/reward intervention can be effective and appreciated among the stakeholders most influenced by the intervention. The choice for an AC4P stained glass window and the students' significant increase in self-esteem throughout the intervention are evidence of its special success.

The Principal told a news reporter, "I think it struck a chord with our students, and would at any school. Actively Caring for People has become part of our language, part of our school."[17]

WHY READ THIS BOOK

Why provide particulars about an AC4P intervention to prevent bullying behavior, including references of relevant research literature? Well, did I get your attention? The empirical presentation of a positive approach to reducing bullying—that also increased students' self-esteem and interpersonal helping—is worth noting. I bet you are interested in creating a positive school culture where interpersonal compassion prevails over interpersonal conflict and bullying—whether you are a teacher, school administrator, parent, or SRO.

It's likely some of you have experienced negative ramifications dealing with destructive school behavior using those efficient top-down punitive consequences. You may have witnessed a temporary decrease in the undesirable behavior targeted by the punitive approach. But the lasting effects from this all-to-common strategy are usually more detrimental than beneficial. Undesired behavior is apt to occur again, behind the backs of school personnel who try to manage behavior with negative consequences; and the attitude and self-esteem of the punished person has likely gone south.

This book teaches an evidenced-based positive process to improve behavior and attitude concurrently, and nurture an AC4P culture that enables students and teachers to look forward to attending class with an optimistic, achievement-focused, and cooperative mindset.

Here are just two real-world examples of AC4P behaviors, examples of Actively Caring that this manual will help you understand and more importantly, promote and support.

STUDENTS FIRST

I gave a wristband to Shawn Wells, Principal at Bollinger Canyon Elementary School. This is a public school that hosts five intensive special-education classrooms for students with autism and other developmental disabilities.

During the past several years, the special-education population at Bollinger Canyon has grown quite a bit, and Shawn has continued to build and support a culture that accepts, understands, and invites special education.

Just a few weeks ago, Shawn designated one of the "staff only" bathrooms to be used for an intensive toilet-training program for a seven-year-old student who was not yet potty trained. This student now successfully uses the toilet on a daily basis for the first time in his life. Additionally, his parents no longer need to spend countless dollars purchasing diapers. Shawn attends and actively participates in nearly all of her student's IEP's and makes frequent visits to the special education classrooms to check in on students and ensure she is familiar with their programs.

With such a large population of special education students, this adds quite a bit of work to Shawn's already busy schedule…but she makes it happen…and she always does it smiling. In my work with Shawn, she has always put the needs of her students first. Thank you Shawn…for Actively Caring about all of your students and their families!! *Wristband #1294*

Joel V.
San Ramon, CA

RECOGNITION IN THE WORST OF TIMES

This past February there was a shooting at my school: Chardon High School. It's been rough for everyone – some more than others. Like many teenagers, I feel as if I'm fighting the world alone, not sure if what I'm fighting for is even right. I just finished track. I'm not a star runner; I'm actually quite slow, but I do it because I enjoy it. The other faster kids are still in season and still being coached.

Anyway, after the shooting my high school received thousands of cards. They mean more to me than any of the other gifts my high school has received. Sadly we must take them down "to move on" as I keep being told. It seems as if half the kids in the school have already forgotten why the cards are there, anyway.

Nevertheless, I feel I need to read the cards just so a person's Actively Caring is not thrown into some box without the slightest thought. I volunteered two times to help take down the cards. Both times I read each one before sorting them into their boxes. I try not to cry but there is no shame in getting teary-eyed.

Of course some of the cards hit home, others made me smile, but in general I feel that after the clean-up I have renewed strength to deal with the confusing mess of feelings.

I can tell myself I did this clean-up for those who wrote the letters, or for the victims of the shooting, or to help the janitor who would have to deal with the thousands of cards, but I did this for me. I wanted to and that's why I did it.

The day I was taking down the cards I was extremely sad. I was thinking how I haven't truly accomplished anything since February. My grades dropped and track was not a particularly successful season for me. The worst part is that my relationships with friends and family are strained. I keep reading the cards, taking the strengths of those individuals who sent them, trying to feel that strength.

Amazingly, my track coach, Bartley, comes up behind me one day and says "You're a good kid, you know that?" I needed to hear those words more than anything. He pulls off his AC4P wristband and gives it to me. I was speechless. This told me I was doing something right. I had always liked and admired him, but this was something more than I ever expected. This is my coach Actively

Caring for me, and I look forward to paying it forward and passing on this wristband. *#47735*

Megan W.
Chardon, OH

These personal stories capture my vision of an educational culture free of illicit drugs, interpersonal conflict and bullying; and self-motivated learning is inspired by self-motivated teaching. This book gives you state-of-the-art principles and applications to achieve this vision.

I am honored to provide you with this first edition of our *AC4P Manual for Schools*. I dedicate this scholarship to all who have chosen to serve our children with the education they need to prosper in an ever more complex and challenging world. I hope you find the time, interest, and passion to answer the questions and conduct the exercises offered throughout this teaching/learning manual. Most importantly, I hope you put your new knowledge of humanistic behaviorism into beneficial action.

Please document your experiences applying the AC4P principles and using this manual, and email me feedback about how to improve the next edition of this teaching/learning guide.

E. Scott Geller
Alumni Distinguished Professor & Director
Center for Applied Behavior Systems
Department of Psychology
Virginia Tech
Blacksburg, VA 24061-0436
esgeller@vt.edu

FROM PRINCIPLES TO APPLICATIONS

Seven research-based lessons from psychology—the science of human experience—are the bedrock for this manual's teaching/learning process. The first four lessons reflect critical behavior-management fundamentals: positive reinforcement, observational learning, and behavior-based feedback. The subsequent three lessons are derived from humanism, but behaviorism or applied behavioral science (ABS) is essential to bring humanistic principles to life. The result—*humanistic behaviorism*—enhances long-term positive and sustainable relations between teachers, students, school administrators, and SROs. It promotes an optimal teaching/learning climate and prevents interpersonal conflict and bullying behavior.[18]

Please take note that optimal training of these seven AC4P lessons calls for relevant role playing and behavioral feedback. "Training" implies that certain information is actually practiced by the learning participants. Improvement-focused behavioral instruction follows. Without action and feedback, a teaching/learning session only amounts to "education" or awareness.

Both education and training are provided in this manual. Each research-based principle for AC4P intervention is explained and followed by questions or scenarios to facilitate group discussion. Behavioral exercises are given to practice each principle and receive supportive and corrective feedback for continuous improvement. Sharing opinions and ideas illustrates the variety of relevant applications derived from just one research-based AC4P principle.

Some of your group discussions will become brainstorming sessions for innovative applications of AC4P principles. When some of these possibilities are practiced via interpersonal role playing with feedback, you have genuine "training" that increases the probability of applying the benefits of AC4P in your school, your home, and throughout your community.

Lesson 1
EMPLOY MORE POSITIVE CONSEQUENCES

Behavior is motivated by consequences. This is the start of our teaching/ learning journey. Dale Carnegie, author of the seminal book: *How to Win Friends and Influence People*, said in 1936, "Every act you have ever performed since the day you were born was performed because you wanted something. [19] We do what we do for one reason: the consequences we expect to get, or escape, or avoid by doing it. This illustration shows, students' learning is benefitted by realizing explicit consequences.

Your own life's journey reflects this fundamental principle from behavioral science. A simple question: Would you rather be influenced by positive consequences or negative consequences? Personal experience and common sense give you the answer, and it's verified by more than 70 years of behavioral research.

What is your reaction to the illustration?

Will the athlete run? Of course he will. People react instantly to avoid an impending negative consequence. But how long will the athlete keep running if his coach is not there to hold him accountable? What will be his attitude about running? Will he be self-motivated to run without an extrinsic accountability system to keep him going?

The critical topic of self-motivation is covered later in this manual, including ways to enhance self-motivation in ourselves and others. For now, just consider the potential unpleasant effects of using the threat of a negative consequence to activate avoidance behavior and the administration of a negative consequence following the occurrence of an unwanted behavior.

For example, I know "command and control" and aloof coaching has caused many students to quit a sport. Too many coaches rely exclusively on corrective feedback, and minimize positive supportive feedback to instruct and motivate athletes. Effective feedback delivery is covered later under Lesson 3.

Following desirable behavior with positive consequences is the most efficient and effective way to improve both behavior and attitude simultaneously. We all know what happens to our attitude when undesirable behavior is followed by a negative consequence? Question: If we know this, *why are negative consequences used more often than positive consequences to improve behavior in school, in sports, at home, in organizations, and throughout communities?*

Please record your answers to this question here and then participate in a group discussion about answers, if possible.

_____

_____

_____

_____

_____

_____

_____

A MATTER OF MINDSET

Your answers reflect this very principle: Behavior change techniques that are most convenient and rewarded with immediate impact are most popular, at least in the short term. But discuss answers to this question: *Which behavior-change technique will have the longest-term benefit? Why?*

_____

_____

_____

_____

_____

_____

Often, you can view the same situation as: a) control by penalizing unwanted behavior; or b) control by rewarding desired behavior. For instance, some of my university students are motivated to avoid failure (i.e., a poor grade); others aspire to achieve success (e.g., a good grade or increased knowledge).

Which students feel more empowered and in control of their grade? Which ones have a better attitude toward class? You know the answers. Just think about the difference in your own feelings or attitudes when you perceived your behavior was being influenced by positive or negative consequences.

Figure 1 depicts four distinct achievement-related person-states that have been researched by behavioral scientists to explain differences in attitude and motivation when working to achieve success versus avoid failure.

Figure 1. Motivational typologies defined by achieving success vs. avoiding failure.

A *success seeker* is the most desirable state. These are resilient optimists who adapt positively to setbacks. Self-confident and willing to take on challenges, success seekers don't evade demanding tasks to avoid failure. They awaken each morning to an *opportunity* clock rather than an *alarm* clock. You can influence this mindset or attitude toward life both in yourself and others by employing situational manipulations and communication, both interpersonal and intrapersonal (i.e., self-talk).

Failure avoiders do not anticipate success and very much dread failure. By any means necessary they will protect themselves from appearing incompetent. They shield themselves from failure by setting the bar low for expectations and using defensive pessimism. Students with this mindset are motivated but "unhappy campers." They say, "I've *got* to go to class; it's a *requirement*," rather than, "I *get* to go to class; it's an *opportunity*."

Discussion Questions

What conversations do you have with others and within yourself (self-talk) that influence success-seeking more than failure-avoiding mindsets, and vice versa?

_____

_____

_____

_____

_____

_____

_____

_____

Bottom line: Applying soon, certain and positive consequences is most effective to improve behavior and attitude at the same time. Employing this life lesson every day is both critical and challenging. Why? We live in a "click-it-or-ticket" culture that relies on negative consequences to control behavior, from the classroom and workplace to our homes, and during our travels in between. Our government's approach to behavior management is to pass a law and enforce it. Who are our society's visible law-enforcement agents?

_____

_____

_____

_____

_____

_____

Discussion Questions

Given the law-enforcement duty of police officers, what attitudes and emotions do you typically associate with school resource officers (SROs)?

_____

_____

_____

_____

_____

Observe SROs at your school and/or at other schools in your community. Share your perceptions of SROs' positive and negative attitudes or emotions. What positive consequences could tip the attitude scale to positive over negative?

_____

_____

_____

_____

_____

_____

Lesson 2
BENEFIT FROM OBSERVATIONAL LEARNING

I f you want to be better at what you do, watch someone who performs that behavior better than you. The power of observational learning is obvious. A large body of psychological research indicates this type of learning is part of almost everything we do.[20]

Our actions influence others more than we realize. Children learn by watching us at home; colleagues are influenced by our actions at work. We're often unaware that we wield this influence. What do children learn by watching the driving behavior of their parents, including their parent's verbal behavior? This illustration shows most parents don't realize how their behavior significantly shapes their children's' actions.

The power of observational learning is illustrated by this poem:

The eye's a better teacher and more willing than the ear;
Fine counsel is confusing, but example's always clear;
And the best of all the preachers are the ones who live their creeds.
For to see the good in action is what everybody needs.
I can soon learn how to do it if you'll let me see it done;
I can watch your hands in action, but your tongue too fast may run;
And the lectures you deliver may be very wise and true.
But I'd rather get my lesson by watching what you do.
For I may not understand you and the high advice you give.
There's no misunderstanding how you act and how you live.
Forrest H. Kirkpatrick

THE PUBLIC VIEW OF SROS

Attitudes about SROs are often influenced by a singular observation of an interaction between a student and an SRO. Or, by a story heard about an interaction between a student and an SRO. SROs have a critical reactive dimension to their job; they are typically involved in negative confrontations with students. Too often the result is apprehending a disruptive student. These types of encounters involving SROs are most likely to be played up by the news media.

SROs, students, and teachers have many more positive than negative interactions, right? It's just that most are never publicized. An exception is when SROs respond to an emergency reported by the media and help those needing assistance. However, a large proportion of the crises reported in the news involve experts from the other helping professions, from fire fighters to healthcare workers.

Controlling crowds and chasing suspects or perpetrators is the most visible role of the SRO in large-scale emergencies or threats to security. These protective behaviors are terribly important, but they do not define an SRO. However, these images do elicit the typical public stereotype of an SRO.

The daily behavior of SROs are actually more proactive than reactive, and involve many more positive than negative interactions with students and teachers. Most of us don't see these positive proactive interactions with SROs, and so we don't learn about the "upside" of maintaining a safe and secure school.

A NEED FOR DISCUSSION

I'm sure you agree with the public's generally negative perception of SROs, based on crisis situations and media reporting. But what's the basis for this understanding? Let's entertain a rationale from personal observational learning. If you are studying this guidebook alone, I suggest you write your answers in the space provided.

1. Are experiences between SROs and students more frequently positive than negative? Justify your answer, which I hope is "yes." Use examples from observational learning, from personal experience, or observations reported by others.

_____

_____

_____

_____

_____

_____

_____

_____

2. How many, if any, of these *positive* exchanges between SROs and students are reported in the news? How can more people learn about these positive interactions, especially through observational learning?

_____

_____

_____

_____

_____

3. List some of the proactive roles expected of SROs, but not typically reported by the news media and not observed by the public.

_____

_____

_____

_____

_____

_____

4. If you are an SRO, how did observational learning influence your decision to become one? In other words, what observed behaviors of SROs, if any, inspired you to become a school resource officer?

_____

_____

_____

_____

_____

5. What particular SRO behaviors have you learned by watching other SROs? Please explain.

_____

_____

_____

_____

_____

_____

_____

Lesson 3

IMPROVE WITH BEHAVIORAL
FEEDFORWARD AND FEEDBACK

P ractice makes perfect" is simply not true. Practice makes permanence. Behavior improves only through the repetition of behavior-focused feedback. Sometimes feedback is a natural consequence—the golfer and tennis player see where their ball lands after swinging a club or racket. But even when we observe an outcome of our behavior, behavioral feedback from an observer (e.g., a coach) is needed to properly adjust and improve our performance.

Students, like everyone, want to be competent at skills they believe are meaningful or worthwhile. Effective student teaching and administration of a school to keep students and teachers safe and secure is certainly worthwhile work. So how can teachers and SROs become more competent?

Relevant behavior-focused feedback is the answer. I'm sure you know this. But who should deliver improvement feedback? This is also obvious: Teachers and SROs need to give each other supportive and corrective feedback.

The letters of COACH capture it all: "C" for Care; "O" for Observe; "A" for Analyze; "C" for Communicate, and "H" for Help, as depicted in Figure 2.

Caring kicks off the coaching process. "Know I *Care* and you'll care what I know. I care so much, I'm willing to *Observe* you and notice the occurrences of desirable (or effective) and undesirable (or ineffective) behavior." Also noted are environmental factors that may influence observed behavior, from classroom conditions to behavioral consequences (e.g., grades). This is the *Analysis* phase of coaching.

Interpersonal *Communication* comes next. How should you deliver information gained from your prior *Observation* and *Analysis* steps? Most students want to improve, but many resist giving and receiving the kind of communication critical for positive behavior change.

Some students and people in general, perceive feedback that requires personal change as an indictment of their current life style, study habits, or diligence. This

Figure 2. The five components of AC4P coaching.

reaction occurs most often when a student is asked to change dramatically, and when current study habits or other behaviors have been embedded for years.

Effective behavior-improvement coaches steer clear of disruptive and dramatic communication to overcome resistance to behavioral feedback. They emphasize incremental fine tuning or successive approximations. They also accentuate the positive—occurrences of desirable behavior—to facilitate behavioral and attitudinal improvement.

Help—the last letter of COACH—is accomplished if interpersonal communication goes well. Behavioral feedback is accepted and is used to improve pinpointed behavior. Note how the four letters of HELP—Humor, Esteem, Listen, and Praise—are all strategies that increase the probability a teacher's advice, directions, or feedback will be appreciated and accepted.

MISUSE OF FEEDBACK

Imagine you receive an email from your Principle requesting that you come to her office at the end of the day to receive some "feedback." How do you feel? Do you envision a "feedback session" with unpleasant verbal communication and emotion? How relevant is this illustration.

Two common characteristics of feedback influence a student's desire to avoid feedback, and justify his or her negative reaction. First, negative or *corrective* feedback typically takes precedence over positive or *supportive* feedback. Many teachers and SROs experience this unfortunate tendency at their school.

In other words, many parents, teachers, coaches, supervisors, and SROs use reprimands more often than praise, with the apparent belief we learn more from our mistakes than our successes. Empirical research and even common-sense indicate this is untrue.

The second reason feedback carries negative baggage is that we often correct others without focusing solely on their behavior. The way feedback is delivered suggests the problem or error observed extends beyond behavior. The child is "sloppy;" the student is "ignorant;" the athlete is "lazy;" the perpetrator is inherently "evil;" or the worker is "careless." This type of judgmental delivery does more harm than good. Substantial research demonstrates dramatic disadvantages of giving labels to people that go beyond their behavior or effort, even when the label is positive.[21]

It's essential to separate behavior from person factors when giving and receiving feedback. Of course this is easier said than done. But corrective feedback should not indict one's personality or indicate a character flaw. Feedback must not relate to an individual's attitude, motivation, competence, or family history. Feedback focuses strictly on observed behavior.

Sure, if a student responds well to supportive or corrective feedback it can lead to improved attitude, motivation, competence, and even a better person-state. But you provide feedback for only one reason: to pinpoint desired and/or undesired behavior. When this is realized by teachers, SROs, school administrators and others who regularly give and receive feedback, the benefits of behavioral coaching are maximized.

There's room for improvement in most everything we do; only by receiving and accepting behavior-based feedback can we do better.

IT'S IN THE DELIVERY

I hope it's clear that giving interpersonal feedback at the right time certainly increases its beneficial impact on behavior. Actually, timing is one of four basic guidelines I recommend you consider when planning your feedback strategies. These rules of feedback delivery are readily remembered with the key words— *Specific, On time, Appropriate, and Real.* Note the first letters spell "soar." Follow these four basics of feedback delivery and you will "soar" to success with interpersonal feedback.

SPECIFIC

As we've discussed, your feedback must focus on specific behavior. As a *consequence* (for motivation), your feedback specifies the behaviors to stop and the behaviors to keep performing. And as an *activator* (or directive), teaching feedback reminds a student to perform a particular task in a certain way. This feedback needs to be given using straightforward and objective words, and is actually *feedforward.*

Figure 3 illustrates the activator-behavior-consequence (ABC) model of ABS. Note the distinction between feedforward and feedback depicted in this diagram. Both of these behavior-improvement techniques need to be understood

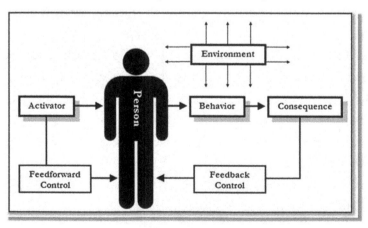

Figure 3. The ABC model of ABS that distinguishes feedforward from feedback.

and accepted. Obviously, students, children, and employees can all misperceive, misunderstand, or deny feedforward or feedback. The principles discussed here suggest ways to ensure that behavioral direction (feedforward) and behavioral support or correction (feedback) are taken in and appreciated.

Ambiguous and subjective language about internal person-states is not useful. In fact, it can be counterproductive. Think about the impact of evaluations that spell out "You're careless, lazy, unenthusiastic, unaware, disorganized, or out-of-touch." These types of statements are resented and lessen the acceptability of the behavioral message. And this is important: When you deliver positive statements, watch for the use of "but."

We often feel obligated to add a negative statement to balance praise or appreciation. "I like the way you clarify concepts with real-world and relevant examples, *but* next time try to be more passionate in your demeanor." This kind of mixed message weakens your feedback. Some people hear only the negative and miss the positive. Others discount both messages, figuring one positive and one negative equals no communication.

Make your specific behavior-focused feedback "short and sweet." Don't combine supportive and corrective feedback in one exchange or overload a person with several behaviors to continue or change. Instead, concentrate your advice on one area of performance. Give people several concise and specific feedback messages, rather than fewer but longer feedback sessions with mixed and potentially confusing motives and directives.

ON TIME

As we've discussed, motivational feedback to increase or decrease how often a behavior occurs should follow the target behavior as soon as possible. An excessive delay between the behavior and the supportive or corrective consequence can be counterproductive, as reflected in the illustration.

On the other hand, if the purpose of behavioral feedback is to shape the quality of a response, it usually makes most sense to deliver this directive feedback

as an activator (i.e., feedforward) preceding the next opportunity to perform the target behavior.

Discussing an error as a consequence can be perceived as punishing and frustrating if an opportunity to correct the observed error does not present itself in the near future. When the opportunity to correct the behavior eventually arrives, the advice might be forgotten. Timing matters. When you time your advice to improve in close proximity to the next opportunity for the desired behavior to recur (i.e., as feedforward), you increase its directive influence and reduce the potential of a negative attitude that results from catching a person making a mistake.

Appropriate. Specific and well-timed feedforward and feedback need to be tailored to the needs, abilities, and expectations of the person receiving direction, support, or correction. Simply put, feedforward and feedback should fit the situation. Both should be expressed in language the performer can understand and appreciate, and communication should be customized for the individual's ability to perform the particular task.

When people learn a task, directive feedforward and motivational feedback need to be detailed and perhaps accompanied with a behavioral demonstration. In these learning situations (i.e., observational learning), it's important to align your advice with the individual's achievement level. Don't expect too much and overload more advice than the performer can grasp in one feedforward exchange.

At times, experienced teachers, school administrators, or SROs exhibit sub-par behavior even when they know how to do the job well. They might have developed sub-optimal habits or are just taking a short-cut for efficiency. To give experienced individuals detailed instructions about the appropriate way to do their job can be insulting and demeaning. In these situations, it's best to give feedforward. Use it as a reminder to take extra time to achieve effectiveness rather than efficiency. You want quality, not expediency. Important: Preceding your reminder with the words, "As you know," increases acceptance of the reminder.

It's important for you as a behavioral coach to size up the situation. Make your specific and timely feedforward or feedback fit the occasion. This is not easy, and requires an up-to-date awareness of the performer's knowledge and skill regarding a certain task. You also need specific knowledge of the optimal ways to perform a task in a given situation. This is why the most effective intra-school coaching usually occurs between school personnel serving on the same team, or at least among those acquainted with each other's job at the same school.

REAL

Interpersonal coaching is most effective when it occurs between team members, because such feedback is often perceived as most genuine and caring. Feedforward and feedback are ineffective if the verbal behavior is viewed as exerting top-down control, or demonstrating superior knowledge, competence, or motivation. Improving and sustaining the competence of team members is the sole reason to give behavioral feedforward or feedback.

Discipline policies in many schools make it difficult for some people to view corrective feedback as caring and supporting. It might be well-intentioned, but the "gotcha" mindset associated with "rule enforcement" can interfere with a Principal's sincere attempt to correct sub-optimal performance.

Corrective feedback is most likely to be received as genuine or "real" when it occurs between peers—teachers, students, administrators, school psychologists, and SROs on the same team. Peers possess the most intimate knowledge of situation and the person(s) involved, and thus have sufficient information and opportunity to make feedforward and feedback specific, on time, appropriate, and real.

IN SUMMARY

We've reviewed key guidelines to deliver effective interpersonal feedforward and feedback. The word "SOAR" is a useful teaching/learning tool, because each letter of this acronym reflects a key word that implicates a rule to deliver feedforward and feedback effectively—**S**pecific, **O**n time, **A**ppropriate, and **R**eal.

"SOAR" indicates the special value of team members giving each other on-the-job feedforward and feedback. Team members have the most complete knowledge of the feedforward/feedback recipient and the situation. They are best positioned to make their behavioral feedforward and feedback: a) *specific* in terms of behavior to initiate, continue or stop; b) *appropriate* for the knowledge, abilities, and experiences of the performer; and c) reflect *real* concern for the individual's competence and job effectiveness.

Members of a team are also most likely to be *on time* with feedforward or feedback, whether their communication serves as an activator, motivator, or both. Whether you use feedback to support desirable behavior or decrease undesirable behavior, "on time" means your feedback should be delivered as a consequence that follows the observed behavior as soon as possible.

In contrast, when using feedforward to encourage behavior (perhaps as a correction for sub-par behavior observed earlier) you should consider your communication a reminder or an activator. Wait for a situation that calls for the particular behavior and then offer a specific, appropriate, and genuine reminder. Appropriate interpersonal feedforward or feedback enables you to "soar" to new heights of teaching, coaching, and SRO effectiveness.

Discussion Questions

It's extremely useful to discuss these four guidelines for giving feedforward and feedback in situations relevant for the participants. The format to connect these principles with realistic applications can vary markedly. An instructor could solicit comments from all participants. Or, participants could be divided into small groups; and after the questions and issues posed here are discussed, a representative from each group could report their perspectives to the entire assembly of participants.

Whatever protocol you employ to encourage an interactive discussion of feedforward and feedback, consider the following questions. In some teaching/learning situations it might be optimal or most convenient for participants to write personal reactions to these questions before discussing them with one or more other participants.

1. What specific situations could be improved using interpersonal feedforward and feedback between school personnel? Is this kind of communication more important in some circumstances than others? Please explain.

_____

_____

_____

_____

2. What factors push back against school personnel giving each other behavior-based feedforward or feedback?

_____

_____

_____

_____

3. How might barriers to giving others behavior-improvement feedforward or feedback be overcome?

_____

_____

_____

_____

4. Discuss personal experiences in which you _received_ behavior-based feedforward and feedback from a colleague. How were these exchanges appropriate or inappropriate in regard to the SOAR guidelines?

_____

_____

_____

_____

_____

_____

5. Discuss personal experiences in which you _delivered_ behavior-focused feedforward and feedback to another person. Were your communications appropriate or inappropriate with regard to the SOAR guidelines?

_____

_____

_____

_____

_____

_____

_____

6. Discuss situations when you give students or parents feedforward and feedback as part of your job.

_____

_____

_____

_____

_____

7. How could your typical feedforward and feedback communications with students and parents improve by applying the SOAR guidelines?

_____

_____

_____

_____

_____

_____

_____

8. What prevents you from holding more effective feedforward and feedback conversations with the students you serve?

_____

_____

_____

_____

_____

_____

_____

Lesson 4

USE MORE SUPPORTIVE
THAN CORRECTIVE FEEDBACK

"We can't learn unless we make mistakes." How many times have you heard this? Yes, it might make us feel better about the errors of our ways. It might provide an excuse for focusing more on other people's failures than on their successes. But nothing could be further from the truth. Behavioral scientists have shown convincingly that success—not failure—produces the most effective learning.[22]

At the start of the last century, Edward Lee Thorndike put chickens, cats, dogs, fish, monkeys, and humans in situations that called for problem-solving. He was studying intelligence. Thorndike systematically observed how these organisms learned. The "Law of Effect" was his term to describe the fact that learning depends upon behavioral consequences.[23] A key finding: Markedly more learning occurred following positive consequences (success) than negative consequences (failure).

To solve a problem, does an error need to occur? You can reflect on your own experiences to answer this question. A pleasant consequence directs and motivates you to continue the behavior. You know what you did to receive the reward, and you're motivated to earn another.

But a negative consequence following a mistake only tells you what not to do. It provides no specific direction for problem solving. You can be frustrated and discouraged when a mistake you make is overemphasized; it could actually de-motivate you to continue the learning process.

Errors are not necessary for learning to occur. In fact, when education or training results in no errors, made possible with certain presentation techniques, learning is a most smooth and enjoyable process.[22] Errors disrupt the teaching/learning process and can lead to a negative attitude, especially if negative social consequences accentuate the mistake. Even subtle reactions to an error—a disappointed face or verbal tone—can increase feelings of helplessness or despair and turn off a person to the entire learning process.

Supportive feedback is the most powerful positive consequence to construct and sustain a successful learning process. It's the theme of this discussion. Still, some attempts to be positive and supportive are ineffective, as this illustration shows. Next, I provide five basic guidelines for giving quality supportive feedback.

BE TIMELY

To provide optimal direction and encouragement, supportive feedback needs to connect directly with the desired behavior, as *not* demonstrated in the illustration. When people know what they did to earn appreciation, they might be motivated to continue that behavior.

If it's necessary to delay the supportive feedback, your conversation should relive the activity deserving recognition. Talk specifically about the behavior that warrants special acknowledgement. Don't hesitate to ask the recipient to recall aspects of the situation and the commendable behavior. This enables you to direct and motivate the person to continue his or her desired behavior.

MAKE IT PERSONAL

Supportive feedback perceived as personal is most meaningful. Your verbal support should not be vaguely generic, applicable for any situation, as in "Nice job!" Customize it to fit a particular individual and circumstance. This happens naturally when the supportive feedback is linked to designated behavior. When you recognize someone, you're expressing personal thanks.

At times, it's tempting to say, "*We* appreciate" rather than "*I* appreciate," and to refer to gratitude of the department rather than *personal appreciation*. But speaking for an organization or company can come across as impersonal and insincere.

It's appropriate, naturally, to reflect a person's value to the organization when you give supportive feedback, but your focus should be personal: "I saw what you did to support the AC4P behavior of that student and I really appreciate it. *Your example demonstrates the kind of leadership we need around here to nurture an AC4P culture of compassion.*" This second statement illustrates the next guideline for giving quality supportive feedback.

TAKE IT TO A HIGHER LEVEL

When your supportive feedback reflects a higher-order quality, it's most memorable and inspirational. Add a universal positive such as leadership, integrity, trustworthiness, or AC4P to your recognition statement and you make your feedback more meaningful and rewarding. It's important to state the specific behavior first, and then make an obvious linkage between the behavior and the positive characteristic it reflects.

Later, we discuss the use of an AC4P wristband to show appreciation for AC4P-related behavior. In these cases, we offer the wristband as a symbol of AC4P leadership, and it's worn to show membership in an elite group of individuals dedicated to cultivating an AC4P culture of compassion. The AC4P wristband not only rewards AC4P behavior, but signifies belongingness and community—participation in a worldwide AC4P Movement.

This is how you bring interpersonal supportive feedback to a higher level of effectiveness, positively impacting the recipient's self-esteem, competence, and sense of interdependence and belongingness. Later we explain how these person-states enhance self-motivation and the propensity to perform more AC4P behavior.

DELIVER IT PRIVATELY

Supportive feedback needs to be delivered privately and one-on-one because it is personal and indicative of higher-order attributes. A certain degree of courage is called for if you are not comfortable in private, one-on-one conversations, especially with people you don't know well. But consider this: Your verbal support is special and only relevant to one person. It is more meaningful and genuine if you deliver it personally—from one caring individual to another.

Recognizing individuals in front of a group is a traditional rite. It is typified in athletic contests and reflects the pop-psychology slogan, "Praise publicly and reprimand privately." Many teachers take their lead from this common-sense statement and recognize their student's in-group settings.

To be held up as an exemplar before one's peers is maximally rewarding, right? Not necessarily. Many people feel embarrassed when singled out in front of a group. This could be out of fear of later harassment by peers. The recognized individual might be degraded as an "apple-polisher" or "brown-noser," or accused of "sucking up to the teacher."

When I was in third grade, my teacher recognized me in front of the class for doing "an excellent job" on my homework. As depicted in the illustration, I was so embarrassed. After school, a gang of fellows gave me a playground beating. Unfortunately, my teacher never learned about this negative consequence of her public recognition.

Athletic performance is measured objectively and winners are determined fairly and duly recognized. But in educational and work settings it's usually impossible to objectively assess everyone's relevant behaviors and obtain a fair ranking for individual recognition. Praising one individual in public may be perceived as favoritism by those who feel they did equally well, but did not get praised. This type of appraisal also sets up a win-lose atmosphere—perhaps appropriate for some sporting contests—but not when your goal is to promote a cooperative interdependent culture of optimal teaching and learning.

It's beneficial, of course, to recognize teams of students for their accomplishments, and this *can* be done in a group setting. Since individual responsibility is diffused or dispersed across the group, there is minimal risk of embarrassing someone or activating peer harassment.

It's important to realize, though, that group achievement is rarely democratic—resulting from the equal input of all team members. Some take the lead and work harder; others "coast" and count on the group effort to make them shine. It's important for you to personally and privately recognize the individuals who go beyond what's asked of them for the sake of their team.

LET IT SINK IN

We live in an accelerated age of doing more with less. So we tend to overcompensate when we finally communicate with a busy person. We recognize someone's special AC4P effort, and then we're tempted to tag on a bunch of unrelated statements, even a request for additional behavior. This comes across as, "I appreciate what you've done, but I need more."

Resist this temptation. Simply praise the AC4P behavior you observed. If you have additional points to discuss, it's best to reconnect later, after your supportive feedback has had a chance to sink in and become part of the individual's self-talk for self-recognition and self-motivation.

You can give people a script to use to reward their own behavior when you give supportive recognition. Supportive feedback strengthens the other person's self-reward system. This positive self-talk (or self-recognition) is critical for long-term maintenance of desired behavior. By allowing your supportive feedback to stand alone and be personally absorbed, you enable internalization of rewarding self-talk that can be used later as self-motivation to perform the recognized behavior again.

USE TANGIBLES FOR SYMBOLIC VALUE

Tangible rewards can detract from the self-motivating aspect of quality recognition. If a material reward is the focus of an AC4P recognition process, words of appreciation are diminished in value. And self-motivation is stifled.

But tangible rewards delivered as tokens of appreciation add to the quality of interpersonal recognition. Rewards that include a relevant AC4P slogan, as found on the AC4P wristband, help promote desired behavior. But remember, how you deliver your tangible reward determines whether it adds or subtracts from the long-term sustainability of your praise.

The benefit of interpersonal recognition is weakened if the tangible reward is seen as a payoff for AC4P behavior. If it is received as a symbol of going the extra mile for another person's well-being, it strengthens your praise. Go ahead, have the courage to tell it like it is: The AC4P wristband or another tangible reward is a token of appreciation or a symbol of going beyond the call of duty.

CONSIDER SECONDHAND RECOGNITION

Up to now, we've discussed one-on-one verbal communication in which you recognize another person for a particular AC4P behavior. You can also do this indirectly, and this approach comes with special advantages. Suppose, for example, you overhear a colleague tell another person of your outstanding presentation about the AC4P Movement. How does this secondhand recognition affect you? Do you believe the words of praise you overheard were genuine?

People can suspect the sincerity of praise when it's delivered face-to-face. Is there some ulterior motive? Perhaps a favor is expected in return, as shown in the illustration. Or perhaps the recognition is devalued because it's

perceived merely as a forced communication exercise. Secondhand recognition is not as easily tainted with these potential biases.

A colleague tells you that someone at your school relayed to her the superb job you did leading a group meeting. What is the impact of this secondhand recognition? Chances are you'll consider it authentic because your colleague only reported what someone else said. Because that person reported your success to your colleague rather than you, no ulterior motive exists for the indirect praise.

Secondhand recognition can build a sense of belongingness or group cohesion among individuals. When you learn someone was bragging about your behavior, your sense of friendship with that person will likely increase.

Talk about the achievement of others in behavior-specific terms and you begin a cycle of positive communication that sustains desired behavior, and activates self-talk that begets self-recognition and self-motivation.

Take it upon yourself to initiate this cycle of positivism. Set an example for the kind of interpersonal communication that enhances self-esteem, self-efficacy, personal control, optimism, and group cohesion. These are the very person-states that increase the potential for more AC4P behavior to occur, and the achievement of an interdependent culture of compassion.[24]

ACCEPT SUPPORTIVE FEEDBACK

Most of us are caught completely off guard when we're acknowledged for our commendable actions. Why? It's because we get so little supportive feedback from others. We don't know how to digest this recognition when it finally comes. Don't shy away when it is delivered; have the courage to embrace it. Remember the basic behavioral-science principle: Consequences influence the behaviors they follow.

As the first lesson explained, positive consequences increase the odds that the recognized behavior will continue. Plus, how you react to supportive feedback influences whether the observer will try to give supportive feedback again. It's crucial to react appropriately when you receive recognition from others. Let's consider seven basic guidelines for receiving supportive behavioral feedback.

DON'T DENY OR DISCLAIM

When we attempt to give supportive recognition, we often get a reaction that implies we're wasting our time. We hear disclaimers such as, "It really was nothing special" or "Just doing my job." The most common reply: "No problem." This implies there was nothing special about the behavior and it didn't warrant supportive feedback.

Supportive feedback must be accepted without any denial or disclaimer; without deflecting credit to others. There's nothing wrong with taking pride in our small-win accomplishments, even if others contributed to the successful outcome. After all, the vision of an AC4P culture calls for everyone performing discretionary behavior on behalf of the well-being of others. In this context, numerous people deserve recognition daily.

Supportive feedback will be intermittent at best for everyone—that's simply reality. So when your turn comes, accept the feedback not only for your recognized behavior, but for many prior desirable behaviors you performed that went unnoticed. Genuinely appreciating supportive feedback increases the chances that the person who gave *you* feedback will give more behavioral recognition to *others*. Plus, you might be inspired to do the same. You realized a personal benefit from the recognition you received, and you want others to experience such positive behavioral support.

LISTEN ACTIVELY

Listen actively to the person who recognizes you with supportive feedback. Certainly, you want to learn what you did right. Plus, you can evaluate how well the supportive feedback is delivered. If the feedback does not pinpoint a particular behavior, you might ask the person, "What did I do to deserve this?" This helps improve the person's method of giving supportive feedback.

Display genuine appreciation for special attention—this is obvious. Consider how difficult it is for many of us to go out of our comfort zone to recognize others with supportive feedback. Relish the fact you're receiving some behavioral recognition, even if its quality could be improved.

USE IT LATER FOR SELF-MOTIVATION

Know that supportive feedback is well-deserved whenever you do receive it. You perform many behaviors when no one else is around. And even when others are present, they are usually so preoccupied with their own routines they don't catch your extra effort.

And relive the moment later. Talk to yourself. Self-recognition can motivate you to keep going as an AC4P agent, doing more than what's expected. Self-talk helps you muster the motivation to perform more of the recognized behavior.

SHOW SINCERE APPRECIATION

Reciprocate with true gratitude. With a smile, a "Thank you," and perhaps special words such as, "You've made my day." How you react to supportive feedback can determine whether that person delivers similar recognition again. Offer words that reflect your pleasure in this memorable positive interaction. Plus, consider the courage the other person might have needed to give you that personal recognition.

I find it natural to add, "You've made my day" to the "Thank you" because it's the truth. When people go out of their way to offer me quality recognition, they *have* made my day. In fact, I typically relive such situations to shine a little light on a later day.

REWARD THE RECOGNIZER

When you accept supportive feedback well, you reward the person for his or her appreciating behavior. This can lead to delivering more positive feedback, especially if the person is more of an introvert and requires boldness to step out and speak up to give recognition.

You can do even more sometimes to assure the occurrence of more supportive feedback. Recognize the person for recognizing you. You might say, for example, "I really appreciate you noticing my behavior and calling me a leader of the AC4P teaching process." Such supportive, rewarding feedback directs and motivates aspects of AC4P teaching that are especially worthwhile and need to become routine.

ASK FOR RECOGNITION

If you feel you deserve supportive feedback, ask for it. Sure, this recognition will come off as less genuine than if it were spontaneous; still the outcome from your request can be quite beneficial. You might hear some words worth reliving later for your own self-motivation. Most importantly, you are reminding the other individual in a polite way that s/he missed a prime opportunity to give supportive feedback. This could be a valuable learning experience for that person.

Say you tell someone else how pleased you are with the outcome of your extra effort. Using the right tone and affect, this verbal behavior isn't bragging but declares your pride in a small-win accomplishment. This is something more people should feel and relive for self-motivation. The other person will surely support your personal praise with their own testimony, and this bolsters your self-motivation. Plus, you teach the other person how to support commendable behavior of others.

THE CRAVING

William James, the first renowned American psychologist wrote, "The deepest principle in human nature is the craving to be appreciated."[25] In 1936, Dale Carnegie advocated "always make the other person feel important" as the key to winning friends and influencing people.[25] How can we satisfy this human need to feel appreciated and important? The answer, of course: Give and receive supportive feedback effectively.

FROM PRINCIPLES TO PRACTICE

Before you apply interpersonal feedback techniques discussed here in the field, I suggest you role-play procedures for delivering supportive and corrective feedback. This role-play should be followed by systematic behavioral feedback from the instructor (and other participants). The delivery of this feedback should adhere to the guidelines presented here, providing observational learning for all participants. I also recommend participants practice recommended feedback techniques on family members before taking their behavior-improvement techniques to the "street."

Work on mastering *supportive* feedback before you attempt *corrective* feedback. It's much easier to deliver supportive feedback, or behavioral recognition, than corrective feedback. It can do no harm even if applied incorrectly. But inappropriate delivery of corrective feedback can result in resistance or hurt feelings on the part of the recipient that can interfere with future interactions.

After discussing the benefits of providing supportive and corrective feedback, the instructor should review the basics of how to deliver and receive effective supportive feedback, as detailed above. Participants should pair off and practice giving each other supportive feedback. One participant should agree to be the feedback "sender" and the other is the "recipient." A particular situation and behavior in a school setting should be defined for the role-play exercise. This can be a real-world situation participants have actually experienced, or only a scenario for delivering feedback.

After receiving supportive feedback, recipients should express their reaction. Did the feedback seem genuine? Did it address a specific behavior? Did the recipient feel rewarded by the exchange? Then the roles should be reversed, with the "sender" playing the role of "recipient" and vice versa.

The instructor/facilitator should circulate among the practicing role-players and note examples of particularly effective and ineffective performance. These observations can then be discussed when the participants reconvene as a group. Group members should discuss their feedback experiences from both the "sender" and the "recipient" perspectives.

Group leaders might select a feedback pair who displays exemplary performance during the role-play sessions and ask them to demonstrate their interaction skills to the rest of the group. The group facilitator might offer supportive and corrective feedback to the presenters, and then ask other participants to contribute their own supportive and corrective feedback.

After you gain confidence through role playing in your ability to "catch good behavior" and give genuine supportive feedback, be ready to reap the benefits of real-world experience. Observe the ongoing behaviors of certain individuals (perhaps starting with your family). After noting a "good" behavior, apply the supportive feedback process. Document your experience by completing the chart. After completing this chart, discuss the information (especially recipient reactions) at group meetings.

Documentation of Delivering Supportive Feedback

Behavior Recognized	Environmental Setting	Reactions of Recipient
1.		
2.		
3.		

4.		
5.		

Role-playing, group demonstrations, and interactive feedback should be used to improve skills of the participants at giving *corrective feedback*. Practice sessions should follow the same basic format as given above for *supportive feedback*, except it will take more practice and individual direction to master this challenging type of verbal communication.

After participants demonstrate with role-playing that they can follow the basics of delivering corrective feedback, they are ready to apply their new verbal skill beyond the classroom. I recommend attempting the first few corrective feedback sessions with family or friends, only after observing an undesired (or less-than-optimal) behavior.

At this point you can move on to delivering corrective feedback techniques for the less-than-optimal behaviors you observe among your work colleagues and/ or your students. For maximum benefit, these sessions should be documented in the chart and discussed in-group meetings among those participating in this ongoing exercise.

Documentation of Delivering Corrective Feedback

Undesirable Behavior	Environmental Setting	Alternative Behavior	Recipient's Reaction
1.			
2.			
3.			
4.			

Finally, it's very useful to practice and document occasions of giving feed*forward* and feed*back* to colleagues and students throughout your day. You should note what went well and not so well when you delivered personal *feedback* for behavioral support or correction. Reflect on these comments as a type of *feedforward* to improve your next opportunity to improve another person's behavior.

I hope you use the chart to systematically document your interpersonal feedforward and feedback experiences. Discuss these feedforward and feedback experiences with others. It's instructive for all as vicarious observational learning (Lesson 2).

Documentation of Feedforward and Feedback Experiences

Feedforward or Feedback	Target Behavior	Situation or Context	Positive Outcome	Room for Improvement

Lesson 5
EMBRACE AND PRACTICE EMPATHY

D ifferent feeling states provoked by positive versus negative consequences are the rationale for using more supportive than corrective feedback to improve behavior. The way you implement a behavior-improvement process can increase or decrease feelings of empowerment, build or destroy trust, and cultivate or inhibit teamwork and a sense of belonging.

Your objective observations of behaviors and subjective evaluations of feeling states should be the basis for your decisions regarding which behavior-improvement process to implement, and how to refine existing intervention procedures. *Empathy* matters. You can use it to evaluate the indirect internal impact of an intervention. Simply imagine yourself in a similar teaching or learning situation. Ask yourself, "How would I feel?"

Empathy is not the same as sympathy, although dictionary definitions are similar. *The New Merriam Webster Dictionary* (1989) defines sympathy as "the capacity for entering into and sharing the feelings or interests of another" (p.727). Empathy is described as "the capacity for experiencing as one's own the feelings of another" (p.248).

Likewise, *The American Heritage Dictionary* (1991) defines empathy as "identification with and understanding of another's situation, feeling, and motives" (p. 449). In contrast, sympathy is "a feeling or expression of pity or sorrow for the distress of another person" (p. 1231). We sympathize when we *express* concern or understanding for another person's situation; we empathize when we *identify* with another's situation.

An empathic level of awareness and appreciation is not easy to achieve. It can be attained only after we minimize those reactive filters that bias our conversations. We must listen intently and proactively. We must hear every word spoken by the other person, and also look for feelings, passion, and commitment. These are reflected as much in body language and manner of expression as in words themselves. The mom in this illustration is not empathic; she isn't listening from the child's perspective.

When you observe another person's behavior, try and view the situation from that individual's perspective. When you hear excuses for inappropriate behavior (e.g., disobeying a school policy), try and see yourself in the same predicament. Imagine what defense mechanisms you might use to protect your own ego or self-esteem. And when you consider action plans for improvement, try and view various alternatives through the eyes of the other person.

Do you think it's difficult to perceive situations and circumstances through the eyes of another? Are you thinking, "This is easier said than done?" Well, you're probably right. But you're only being asked to take a different perspective into your conversations. Approach your coaching conversations with an empathic mindset.

AC4P EMPATHIC LISTENING

Sometimes, Teachers, SROs, coaches, parents, and supervisors offer feedforward directions and corrective feedback in a top-down, controlling manner. Why? It's their eagerness to make things happen. It's passion—the drive to make a difference. The result can be an overly directive approach to get others to change their behavior. Being indirect or nondirective when giving advice is usually more effective, especially over the long term. This is a basic tenant of humanistic therapy.

Think about it: How do you respond when someone tells you precisely and in detail what to do? Who is giving that directive is a factor, but I bet your reaction is not entirely positive. You might follow the instruction, especially if it comes from someone with power—the clout to control consequences. Still, how do you feel? Are you self-motivated to make a lasting change? Perhaps yes, if you had asked for direction, advice or feedback. But if you didn't, you might be insulted or embarrassed. Be more nondirective when you converse to affect behavior change. Being nondirective requires empathic listening.

Dale Carnegie wrote about the value of empathic listening more than 80 years ago in his classic book: *How to Win Friends and Influence People*[25]. His wisdom is reflected in the writing of many authors of popular self-help books, including Stephen Covey's fifth habit of highly effective people, "Seek First to Understand… Then to be Understood."[26]

The same basic strategies for empathic listening are outlined by Carnegie, Covey, and others. If you've had any training in effective communication, you've heard the same advice. Let's review these guidelines with four easy-to-remember words, each beginning with the letter "R."

This gives you a mnemonic to remember how to listen with an empathic AC4P mindset and teach others to do the same. Today, there is a dire need to teach and use these humanistic guidelines for one-on-one empathic listening. Just consider the ever-increasing "lean and mean" and "win/lose" paradigms of contemporary organizations, as well as our fixation on impersonal emails and text messages.

REPEAT

This is the easiest technique. Simply mimic or restate what you hear someone telling you. This clarifies that you heard correctly, and most importantly, it prompts the person to continue speaking. After all, the purpose of empathic listening is to motivate the other person to say more so you can truly come to terms with the issue.

Say a friend tells you he's dropping out of school. You might repeat, "You're dropping out?" You're attentive and interested, and waiting for more information. Reflecting on how drastic the statement sounds, the person might alter course: "Well, at least I feel like dropping out." Following the "repeat" technique, you reply, "You mean you feel like dropping out?" Or you might use different words to echo the same meaning. This is the next empathic listening technique.

REPHRASE

Instead of simply mimicking, you might try rephrasing. In our example, you might say, "You mean you don't like the life of a college student anymore?" By expressing the statement in your own words, you show genuine interest, and you're probing for more information. You're also verifying understanding. When you rephrase what someone else says correctly, you demonstrate caring—you have received and interpreted the communication accurately.

Rephrasing also gives the other person a chance to correct a miscommunication, or a misperception on your part. This is what you seek—an expanded disclosure of the problem. Your friend might clarify, "Well, it's not that I don't like being a student here, it's just that some of my teachers get me so frustrated at times, I feel like quitting."

Now you're on to something. Your friend has revealed a more specific explanation and you respond with, "Your teachers get you frustrated." Or you could *rephrase*: "You mean some of your teachers get you so angry that your motivation to continue attending classes is sapped." Perhaps now you need the next "R" of empathic listening—*ratification*.

RATIFY

Here you demonstrate affirmation or support for another's statement by confirming that you understand. Your ratifying words demonstrate approval for what is being said. This in turn encourages more explanation.

You might assert your approval by saying, "I know the feeling; I've been frustrated with some of my teachers at times and wonder whether this college life is for me."

Here it's tempting to jump in with probing questions to discover more about the frustration, the teachers, or the situation. What teachers got you so upset? What did they do? Why are you so frustrated that you want to quit? Resist this temptation to direct the conversation. You probably don't know enough about the problem to begin a structured (and unbiased) analysis.

Continued empathic listening might reveal problems beyond the teachers. Perhaps it's not a teacher per se, but a particular homework assignment or exam grade. Or the problem might stem from interactions with another student, a family issue, or from feelings of personal inadequacy, including a perceived loss of confidence, self-efficacy, or personal control.

Let's be clear: A person's distress signals can emanate from many sources, and it takes time for the roots to surface in one-to-one conversation. Plus, if the true causes of a problem are disclosed early, it's unlikely you can give optimal advice at this point—directive action that is both useful and accepted. Usually, the best you can do is listen actively with repeat, rephrase, and ratify strategies to flush out the problem. Ultimately, you want the person to express sincere feelings. This is indicated by the fourth "R" word.

REFLECT

When people reflect on their inner feelings about a predicament, frustration or other situation, they discover the heart of the problem. This self-disclosure of person-states can give insight (for both the speaker and the listener) into the true nature of the problem. Now strategies to intervene present themselves. But even with outer layers of the onion peeled away, it's usually better to allow the speaker to contemplate a variety of possible interventions.

If you've been patient, sensitive and emotionally intelligent—an empathic listener—you might receive the ultimate reward. The speaker asks you for specific advice. When you hear questions such as, "What do you think I should do?" you have mastered empathic listening. You have shown you actively care. Now your thoughtful direction will be most relevant, understood, and accepted.

ASK QUESTIONS FIRST

Suppose the conversation is not about a serious issue like personal distress, frustration, or apathy, but simply about a less-than-desired behavior. You see an opportunity for a person to show more or better AC4P behavior in a particular circumstance. What do you say?

Don't direct the person what to do. Get the individual to tell you, in his or her own words, what s/he could have done to be more effective from an AC4P mindset. Ask questions with a sincere and empathic demeanor. Avoid at all costs a sarcastic or demeaning tone.

First, point out certain desirable behaviors you noticed—it's important to start with positives. Then move on to the less desirable behavior. Ask, "Could you have been more effective in that situation?" Of course you hope for more than a "yes" or "no" response to your question. If that's all you get, you need more precise follow-up questioning.

You might point out a particular situation where the behavior you observed could have been more effective. Ask what that behavior should be. We're talking here about giving corrective feedback, as we addressed in the prior lesson. Now you realize the value in starting corrective feedback with questions.

You always learn something by asking questions. If nothing else you'll hear the rationale behind the undesired or sub-optimal behavior. You might uncover a barrier to optimal behavior which you can help the person overcome. A conversation that entertains ways to remove obstacles that hinder desired behavior is especially valuable if possibilities become feasible as relevant action plans.

Patience is obviously required for *empathic* listening, diagnosing, and action planning. Conversations at this level are often lengthy and not efficient, but they are always most effective. Take the time to question and listen to learn first what it's like to be in the other person's shoes. Your objective then shifts to develop a corrective approach fit for the circumstances as mutually understood by everyone in the conversation. If a commitment to follow through with a specific action plan is reached, you were an AC4P behavioral coach.

FROM PRINCIPLES TO PRACTICE

I've reviewed the rationale for empathy, and offered guidelines to accomplish empathic listening. You've been educated. You understand the value and purpose of empathetic listening. Can you be an effective empathic listener in the real world? Of course you can, but it may take some practice, along with relevant behavioral feedback. This is *training*. I suggest the following group exercise:

Divide participants into pairs and ask them to find a relatively quiet location for a brief, quiet conversation. If the size of the group and/or the facility prevents this, simply ask participants to turn to the individual closest to them and execute this practice/feedback session on the spot. Focused on their "private" one-to-one conversations, participants will readily tune out verbal noise from other pairings.

Tell participants this exercise has two trials (if time permits). For the first trial, one member of the dyad (or pairing) serves as the initial speaker; the other will be the empathic listener. For the second trial, the dyadic partners switch roles. For each trial, the speaker tells the listener a personal story, perhaps one that could benefit from another person's perspective and/or advice. Emphasize that the speakers will have a maximum of three minutes to tell their story, while the listeners practice the four R-word guidelines for empathic listening: Repeat, Rephrase, Ratify, and Reflect.

After the three-minute story, listeners should take a maximum of two minutes to offer his/her viewpoint and advice (if relevant), while the former speaker plays the role of empathic listener. Afterward, have each member of the dyad offer behavioral feedback regarding the demonstration of effective vs. ineffective listening skills. Start with supportive feedback and then offer some corrective feedback. Your challenge: Practice the recommended ways of giving and receiving supportive and corrective feedback.

When considering the nature of feedback to give the listener, ask yourself these questions:

1. How did the listener facilitate continued verbal behavior from the speaker?

_____

_____

_____

_____

_____

2. What did the listener do to enable the speaker to reveal personal aspects of his/her story?

_____

_____

_____

_____

3. Did the speaker ask for advice or did the listener offer advice without a request?

_____

_____

_____

_____

4. Was the advice relevant and/or useful?

_____

_____

_____

_____

5. What particular R-word guidelines for empathic listening were used in this dyadic communication?

_____

_____

_____

_____

_____

6. What could the listener have done to facilitate more revealing communication from the speaker?

_____

_____

_____

_____

_____

_____

7. How did this exercise help you appreciate the value of empathic listening, and perhaps realize the validity of the earlier statement, "This is not easy"?

_____

_____

_____

_____

_____

_____

The instructor should call "Time" after the three-minute story, and also after the two-minute reaction by the listener. Then allow five minutes of feedback discussion among the dyads. Total time for Trial 1: ten minutes. If time permits, repeat this entire exercise with the speakers and listeners switching roles (i.e., Trial 2).

After the dyads complete one or two trials, the instructor should facilitate a group discussion about the take-a-ways from this exercise. Ask participants to report what they learned about empathic listening from their discussions. What R-word strategies did they notice, and what were advantages, if any, of practicing these listening techniques?

_____

_____

_____

_____

_____

In what ways, if any, did this experience influence your intentions (i.e., feedforward) for subsequent communication with students, work colleagues or family members? [Note: As you know, when people make a public commitment to improve, the probability of actual improvement increases markedly.]

_____

_____

_____

_____

_____

Lesson 6

DISTINGUISH BETWEEN MANAGING BEHAVIOR AND LEADING PEOPLE

M anagement is not the same as leadership. Yes, both are critically important to draw the best out of people. Simply put, managers hold us *accountable* to perform desirable behavior and avoid undesirable behavior. Leaders *inspire* us to hold ourselves accountable to do the right thing.

Managers control behavior with an external (or extrinsic) accountability intervention or system. Leaders cultivate self-motivation by influencing person-states (e.g., perceptions, attitudes, and/or emotions) that lead to self-motivation. Self-motivation (or self-directed behavior) often leads to *discretionary* behavior— behavior that goes beyond the call of duty.

SELF-MOTIVATION

The C-words of *Choice, Competence,* and *Community* illustrate the three evidence-based perceptions or person-states that determine self-motivation.[27] Dispositional, interpersonal, and environmental conditions that enhance these states increase one's perception of self-motivation. Consider how proper application of the first five lessons can increase perceptions of competence and fuel self-motivation. Consider, too, how language can affect each of these perceptions.

WATCH YOUR LANGUAGE

Your language should exert minimal external pressure. The common phrases: "Safety is a condition of employment," "All accidents are preventable," and "Bullying is a rite of passage," reduce one's sense of autonomy. In contrast, the slogan, "Actively caring is a core value of our organization" implies personal authenticity, interpersonal relatedness, and human interaction.

The popular phrase "random acts of kindness" doesn't suit the description or promotion of AC4P behavior. Random implies behavior happens by chance—it's beyond an individual's choice or control. A kind act might appear random to the recipient, but it was probably performed intentionally out of altruistic motives. Here's an alternative: "intentional acts of kindness."

Language makes a difference. How we prescribe or describe behavior influences our perceptions of its value and relevance to our lives. Language impacts culture, and vice versa.

OPPORTUNITIES FOR CHOICE

Participative management means employees enjoy personal choice during the planning, execution, and evaluation of their jobs. People need a sense of autonomy, regardless of dispositional and situational factors. But in a workplace, managers often tell subordinates what to do rather than involve them in decision-making. We come back to the importance of language again. Should managers give "mandates" or set "expectations"? Should they require "compliance" or request "commitment"?

In schools, students are often viewed as passive learners. It's the teachers who plan, execute, and evaluate most aspects of the teaching/learning process. A student's perception of choice is limited. But when students contribute to the selection and/or the presentation of lesson material, you have cooperative teaching/learning—a most beneficial approach to teaching and learning over the long term.

The same can be said for the role of an SRO who uncovers a specific security issue within a school. A supervisor *(or manager)* directs the SRO on exactly how to handle the issue. In contrast, a *leader* allows the SRO to suggest and plan a course of action.

INVOLVE THE FOLLOWERS

In education settings, autonomy or the perception of choice is supported when rules are established by soliciting input from those affected by the regulation. Teachers and students are more likely to comply with regulations they help define. Shouldn't they have substantial influence developing policy they will be asked to follow? Participants in the classroom know best what actions should be avoided versus promoted to optimize the teaching and learning.

Similarly, before a policy or regulation is implemented in an organization, those affected (i.e., faculty, students, SROs, parents) certainly should have opportunities to offer suggestions. Shouldn't SROs taxed with enforcing security-related policy provide input into behavioral definitions of infractions, as well as enforcement procedures?

EMPOWERMENT

In the management literature, empowerment typically refers to delegating authority or responsibility, or to sharing decision-making. But when a manager says, "I empower you," s/he usually means, "Get 'er done." As reflected in this illustration, the message is, "Make it happen; no questions asked."

In contrast, the AC4P leader first assesses whether the "empowered" individual feels empowered. "Can you handle the additional assignment?" This assessment of feeling empowered involves asking three questions derived from social learning theory.

As depicted in Figure 4, the first question, "Can I do it?" asks if the empowered individual or group has the resources, time, knowledge and ability to handle the assignment. The knowledge and ability components refer to training, and the term *self-efficacy* places the focus on personal belief.

You might think an individual has the competence to complete a task, but the so-called empowered person might beg to differ. A "yes" answer to the first empowerment question by those who receive the assignment or who set a performance-improvement process goal shows that they believe in their own personal effectiveness.

The second question is the response-efficacy question. It asks if those who are empowered believe pursuing and accomplishing the assignment or attaining the process goal (i.e., performing the required behaviors) will contribute to a valued mission of the organization, work team, or individual.

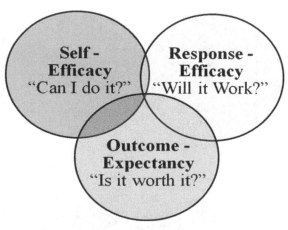

Figure 4. The three beliefs that determine empowerment.

Regarding AC4P instruction, this translates into believing a particular interdependent teaching/learning strategy (e.g., students are rewarded for mentoring other students) contributes to everyone's learning and motivation. Yes, it will work.

A sports team answers "yes" to this

question when athletes believe a new workout routine or competition strategy will increase the probability of winning. Yes, it will work. And a student studying for an exam gives a "yes" answer to response-efficacy if s/he believes the study strategy will contribute to earning a higher exam grade. The long-term behavioral outcome of these two examples can be something more distant and substantive, such as having a winning season or obtaining a college degree.

A "no" answer to the "self-efficacy" question indicates a need for more training. Still, people might believe they can accomplish a particular process or task (i.e., be self-effective), but they might not believe this accomplishment makes a difference in a desired outcome (i.e., response-efficacy). In this case, education is needed, including an explanation of an evidence-based principle or theory and perhaps presentation of convincing data.

The third empowerment-assessment question targets motivation. Is the expected outcome worth the effort? The performance of relevant behavior is motivated by anticipating a positive consequence to achieve or a negative consequence to avoid. Refer back to the first lesson and recall that people feel more choice and are more likely to be self-motivated when they perceive they are trying to achieve a positive consequence, as opposed to avoiding a negative consequence.

EMPOWERING GOALS

Behavior-focused goal setting facilitates individual and/or group success. It's an activator of process activities aimed at achieving a particular outcome. Perhaps you're aware of a popular acronym used to define the characteristics of an effective goal: SMART. Actually a few variations exist of the words reflected by these acronym letters, with *M* representing Measurable or Motivational, and *T* referring to Timely or Trackable, for example.

I propose these acronym words: *S* for Specific, *M* for Motivational, *A* for Attainable, *R* for Relevant, and *T* for Trackable, and the addition of an *S* for Shared (i.e., SMARTS). I add that last *S* because social support can increase commitment to reaching a goal. Please note the connection between SMARTS goals and the empowerment model discussed above.

SMARTS goals empower people because they are *attainable* ("I can do it".), *motivational* ("It's worth it."), and *relevant* ("It will work."). This connection makes it clear that both empowerment and goal setting are similar behavioral antecedents, setting the stage (or activating) certain behavior(s). Each of these activators of behavior defines motivation as anticipating a desired consequence or outcome. Verbal behavior that contributes to goal setting or feelings of empowerment is considered *feedforward,* as we discussed earlier.

EMPOWERMENT VS. SELF-MOTIVATION

Let's consider a critical distinction between these two person-states. Empowerment is a behavioral antecedent (i.e., feedforward); self-motivation reflects the impact of consequences (i.e., feedback). Feeling empowered means an individual is ready (or activated) to work to achieve a given goal. A self-motivated person anticipates or has received a consequence (e.g., feedback) supporting self-directed rather than other-directed behavior.

Consequences that reflect personal choice, competence, and/or a sense of social support or community should enhance self-motivation, and increase the sustainability of a behavior-change intervention that applies positive consequences (Lesson 1). An intervention applying positive consequences to increase the occurrence of a target behavior has longer-term impact if it inspires self-motivation by linking behavioral consequence(s) with a perception of choice, competence, and/or community.

Figure 5 illustrates how empowerment, vision, and goal setting align with the ABC (activator-behavior-consequence) model discussed earlier in Lesson 3. Here's the simple but critical point: A vision and a goal are not enough to sustain desirable behavior. People need to feel empowered to work toward achieving a goal. This includes anticipating the acquisition of desirable consequences and/or the avoidance of undesirable consequences.

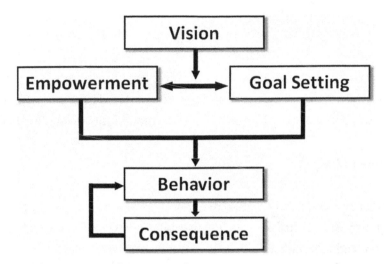

Figure 5. The connection between goal setting, empowerment, and consequences.

Participants need to buy into and own the vision. They need encouragement from peers to attain process goals supporting the vision. Peers also need to give supportive and corrective feedback to increase the quantity and improve the quality of behaviors consistent with those vision-relevant goals. Behavioral consequences are absolutely critical. Empowerment and goal setting can activate desired behavior, but without consequences that are relevant and supportive the behavior won't last. It will extinguish.

Pause For a Review and Discussion

At this point, you could review the key components of this lesson (self-motivation, empowerment, and goal setting) by watching a 15-minute TEDx talk on YouTube. Simply Google Scott Geller TEDx and watch a spirited presentation of the basic concepts introduced in this section.

Afterward, the instructor should facilitate a discussion involving answers to the following questions. Participants could write personal answers to the questions, or divide into smaller interactive groups and discuss answers among themselves before presenting sub-group reports to the entire group. Or the instructor could facilitate constructive discussion of answers to the discussion questions.

Whatever format you choose, your objective is to activate interaction and engagement. You want participants to express their viewpoints and verbalize connections between the self-motivation concepts and their own life experiences.

Discussion Questions

1. Explain the three beliefs that determine empowerment as a person-state, and connect each belief to ways to increase empowerment through training, education, and motivation.

_____

_____

_____

_____

_____

_____

_____

2. Explain the three perceptions (i.e., C-words) that influence self-motivation and provide examples from personal experience.

_____

_____

_____

_____

_____

_____

3. Explain the meaning of B. F. Skinner's legacy: "selection by consequences."

_____

_____

_____

_____

_____

_____

4. Distinguish between a "goal" and a "vision" with a personal example.

_____

_____

_____

_____

_____

5. The ABC Model of behavioral science presumes behavior is _directed_ by activators (or feedforward) and _motivated_ by consequences (e.g., feedback). How can goal setting provide both direction and motivation?

_____

_____

_____

_____

_____

6. Explain the difference between independence and interdependence in terms of optimizing the output of a school or work culture and bringing out the best in students and staff.

_____

_____

_____

_____

_____

_____

7. Which of the lessons in this brief talk on self-motivation were most meaningful to you? Please explain why.

_____

_____

_____

_____

_____

_____

Lesson 7

PROGRESS FROM SELF-ACTUALIZATION TO SELF-TRANSCENDENCE

T he hierarchy of needs proposed by humanist Abraham Maslow is the most popular theory of human motivation. A series of universal needs are arranged hierarchically, and it's presumed we don't attempt to satisfy our needs at one stage or level until our needs at the lower stages are satisfied.

We are first motivated to fulfill basic physiological needs. We require food, water, shelter, and sleep for our very survival. After these needs are met, we want to feel secure and safe from future dangers. When we prepare for future physiological needs, we work proactively to satisfy our need for safety and security.

Our social-acceptance needs come next. We need to have friends and feel as though we belong. When our needs are gratified here, our concern shifts to self-esteem. We are motivated to develop self-respect, gain the approval of others, and achieve personal success. Now we have "self-actualization," right? Does "self-actualization" sit at the top of Maslow's Hierarchy of Needs? No, it does not.

THE HIGHEST NEED LEVEL

Maslow's Hierarchy of Needs is illustrated in Figure 6. You'll note self-actualization is not the highest level need. Maslow revised his renowned hierarchy shortly before his death in 1970, placing self-transcendence above self-actualization.[28] Transcending the self means you go beyond self-interest to actively care for others.

Scant research supports this ranking of human needs in a hierarchy. Intuitively we can accept that various self-needs are to be taken care of before self-transcendent or actively-caring-for-people (AC4P) behavior is likely to occur. But it's possible to think of many individuals performing AC4P behaviors before satisfying all of their personal needs. Mahatma Gandhi put the concerns of others before his own. He was imprisoned, suffered extensive fasts, and eventually was assassinated in his fifty-year struggle to help his downtrodden compatriots.

Figure 6: Maslow's revised hierarchy with self-transcendence at the top.

The need hierarchy connects to various rewarding consequences, and relates to self-motivation and sustaining the impact of a behavior-improvement intervention. Our position in the hierarchy certainly determines what types of consequences are likely to be most rewarding for us at a particular time. If we go without food, shelter, or sleep, for example, we'll focus our efforts on satisfying these basics of survival. But after we meet our need for self-preservation, our motivation requires consequences related to higher-level needs.

Ascending Maslow's hierarchy, we reach need states that implicate consequences linked to self-motivation. For example, consequences that boost our sense of connection with others (i.e., community) satisfy our need for acceptance or social support; consequences that certify our belief that we are competent to perform worthwhile work are associated with the self-esteem and self-actualization needs. Plus, it's intuitive that reaching beyond our own self-needs to help others through AC4P behavior contributes to satisfying our need for social acceptance and self-esteem, and even self-actualization.

Question: When is our quest for social acceptance, self-esteem, and self-actualization met? At what point are we satiated on consequences linked to these need states? Indeed, these are rhetorical questions. I pose them to reiterate the value of delivering rewarding consequences that reflect the three C-words of self-motivation (i.e., Competence, Choice, and Community). These three C-words enhance need states in Maslow's hierarchy that are difficult to satiate.

Bottom line: Behavioral consequences that foster perceptions of our own personal competence, self-worth, interpersonal belongingness, and/or autonomy also facilitate our self-motivation and self-directed behavior. These consequences are likely to have a longer-term impact on us than consequences unrelated to these person-states.

Discussion Exercise

It's helpful to discuss practical answers to the critical question implied above: What kinds of behavioral consequences support or enhance your personal perceptions of choice, competence, and community on the job?

_____

_____

_____

_____

_____

_____

In many cases, how supportive feedback is verbally delivered (as discussed earlier) can influence the recipient's self-motivation. Specify below the verbal support you give to others or receive from others that connect to the beneficial C-words of self-motivation: Choice, Competence, and Community.

_____

_____

_____

_____

_____

_____

THE AC4P MOVEMENT

Most of us care about the well-being of others, but relatively few of us "act" on our feelings of caring. The challenge: Activating and motivating ourselves and others to *actively care*—to take effective action based on our caring?

Our vision: A brother/sister keepers' culture in which we all look out for each other's safety, security, and well-being—we routinely go above and beyond the call of duty for the health, safety, and/or welfare of others. We are "Actively Caring for People" AC4P.

Can teachers, students, and SROs nurture interpersonal empathy, compassion, and AC4P behavior? Wearing the AC4P wristband signifies your support of the AC4P Movement. When you reward the desirable behavior of another person with an AC4P wristband, you promote and enhance the AC4P Movement.

Discussion Questions

1. What are some behaviors a teacher, student, or SRO might observe in others at your school that warrant the reward of an AC4P wristband?

_____

_____

_____

2. What do you say to a person when rewarding an AC4P behavior with an AC4P wristband?

_____

_____

_____

_____

_____

You should be very specific about defining the desirable AC4P behavior you observe and appreciate. Hand the wristband to the individual as recognition for setting an AC4P example. Give the wristband with words that connect to a higher-level need. Don't suggest or even imply that the wristband is a "pay-off" for AC4P behavior. That's never the reason. The wristband is a token of appreciation for the "special servant leadership exemplified by the act of kindness I observed."

Tell the person s/he is now one of many who have joined the AC4P Movement—a flourishing worldwide effort to cultivate cultures of interpersonal compassion and interdependent AC4P behavior.

Proceed to explain the SAPS Process: See, Act, Pass, Share, so the individual is motivated to continue the AC4P process. Tell the person to *See* someone who is looking out for the welfare of another. Then, *act* to recognize and reward this person for the AC4P behavior you observed with an AC4P wristband. Say you are passing on your AC4P wristband for the kind act you just witnessed. Finally, ask the individual to pass the wristband to another person s/he observes performing an AC4P behavior.

Please ask this wristband recipient and new member of the AC4P Movement to *share* this positive exchange on the Internet at www.ac4p.org. Register the number of the wristband, and briefly describe the AC4P behavior that led to the delivery of the AC4P wristband. When this wristband is passed on, a new AC4P story is posted on the AC4P website, along with the particular wristband number.

In this way, positive gossip is spread at your school and beyond. Others see that acting beyond one's self-serving interests on behalf of another person is more common than imagined. AC4P storytelling contributes to make AC4P behavior a social norm. It creates and nurtures a culture of interpersonal trust, compassion, and routine AC4P behavior.

To be sure, the SAPS process is much easier said than done. Why? Actively caring behavior is not part of our normal routine, and it's not expected of us—especially from an SRO. We do not normally look for desirable behavior to reward, even though this is the most powerful way to improve behavior (Lesson 1). In fact, we commonly deny even a "thank you" given for a kind act with expressions like, "No problem," "Don't worry about it," "Just doing my job."

Receiving an AC4P wristband from a teacher or SRO should be very rewarding and memorable. Whenever the AC4P concept is explained to others, it's always appreciated; and whenever an AC4P wristband is offered, it's always accepted with a sincere smile and worn with a sense of pride. I know many individuals who wear their AC4P wristband every day, and actually resist passing it on.

Imagine an individual receiving an AC4P wristband from a teacher or SRO who gives a gracious and tactful description of the AC4P behavior that justified this recognition. Rare and unexpected recognition is sure to be accepted with pleasant surprise. In turn, this wristband recipient will tell friends and family about this very positive and unique encounter at school.

As these positive exchanges among teachers, students, and SROs at school accumulate, the media will take note and report the positive news about the AC4P Movement. The AC4P Movement then spreads throughout the community, and school personnel are identified as the agents of this research-based approach for promoting acts of kindness—actions that promote an optimal teaching/learning culture and deter interpersonal conflict and bullying.

FEEDFORWARD AND THE SAPS PROCESS

The AC4P wristband and SAPS process are essentially a feedback process to show appreciation and reward AC4P behavior of others.

Teachers and SROs search out AC4P behavior from students and other school personnel. When they observe this behavior, they immediately seize the opportunity to reward the AC4P behavior and solicit another participant for the AC4P Movement. Question: How often do you have an opportunity to actually observe AC4P behavior in situations where it's convenient or at least feasible to deliver an AC4P wristband and the AC4P Movement message?

Many people tell me they do not often observe AC4P behavior; when they do, it's frequently not socially convenient or appropriate to reward that behavior on the spot. This might be particularly the case for teachers and SROs who spend most of their workdays serving students, rather than the reverse.

I find myself in situations every day where someone treats me or someone else with an act of kindness. I then conveniently take an AC4P wristband off my wrist and pass it on. But this type of interaction requires practice. I'm often in an environment (e.g., a university campus) where AC4P behavior is relatively easy to observe, and it's convenient to reward this behavior with an AC4P wristband. This might not be the case at your school.

Here's an alternative approach to distributing AC4P wristbands and promoting the AC4P Movement. Deliver an AC4P wristband as feedforward rather than feedback. Consider giving AC4P wristbands to students after you perform an AC4P behavior *for* them.

After a student thanks you for your AC4P behavior on behalf of his or her learning, safety, security, or well-being, follow up by passing on an AC4P wristband and ask the student to join the AC4P Movement. You might say something like:

> *Thank you for appreciating the positive behaviors performed by personnel at our school. Wouldn't it be nice if all of us performed more acts of kindness*

on behalf of others? In fact, the teachers and SROs at our school have joined an Actively Caring for People initiative, or the AC4P Movement, to spread positive behavior between people nationwide, and actually worldwide. This wristband reflects this Movement and I hope you will wear it and join us.

Every wristband is engraved with its own ID number. I will record the ID number on the wristband I've given you when I report this AC4P event on the AC4P Website. Will you also report my act of kindness, along with the ID number on your wristband? The Website address is engraved on the wristband, or you can use the abbreviation: ac4p.org.

I hope you will look for opportunities to pass on your wristband, either after you perform an act of kindness for another person, or when you see another person help someone else. In the first case, you acknowledge your own act of kindness, as I did with you; in the second scenario, you reward someone for his or her AC4P behavior.

Of course, this quotation is only a suggestion. You might certainly discover another way to express three key points: 1) Explain why you passed on the AC4P wristband to the beneficiary of your AC4P service; 2) Introduce the AC4P Movement and the reporting of AC4P stories at the AC4P Website, along with the ID number on the wristband; and 3) Encourage this new member of the AC4P Movement to pass on the wristband when s/he performs an act of kindness (as feedforward) or when s/he observes an AC4P act from another person (as feedback).

Discussion Question

After explaining this feedforward approach to passing on an AC4P wristband, discuss any perceived benefits of this process, other than having an opportunity to explain the AC4P Movement and pass on an AC4P wristband. How can this feedforward practice generate more AC4P behavior? Jot down some possibilities here, and then discuss various answers among colleagues or workshop participants.

_____

_____

_____

_____

_____

_____

PSYCHOLOGICAL IMPACT OF FEEDFORWARD

Lessons 1 and 3 covered the rationale and benefits of rewarding people for their AC4P behavior. Simply put, this feedback can boost self-esteem, personal competence, and a sense of community or belongingness; and it increases the likelihood of an individual performing another act of kindness. Plus, you help that person "bask in the reflected glory" of reaching the highest level of Maslow's Hierarchy of Needs—self-transcendence (Lesson 7).

But what about the feedforward method? What is the psychological impact of giving someone an AC4P wristband after you have helped that person? Let's consider the social influence *Principle of Reciprocity.*

Many people feel a need, even an obligation, to pass on a good turn after receiving one from another person, according to much research evidence provided by social psychologists.[29] When possible, the favor is returned to the original benefactor. But when this is impossible, as when a stranger contributes an AC4P behavior, the beneficiary of the kind act can satisfy the need to reciprocate by helping someone else, even a total stranger.

The reciprocity norm and related research suggest the AC4P feedforward wristband influences the recipient to perform an AC4P act. As the illustration indicates, the "pay-back" from this social influence principle is not always positive, and a lengthy time delay may exist between the behavioral exchange.[29]

The social influence *Principle of Consistency* is also relevant here.[29] People want to be consistent in their actions and attitudes. This research-supported principle indicates it's possible to *act a person into a certain attitude (or way of thinking), and vice versa.* When people perform an act of kindness and/or pass on an AC4P wristband, their positive thoughts and attitudes about the AC4P Movement get a boost.

Every time a teacher or SRO distributes an AC4P wristband as feedforward or as feedback, a deposit is made in his/her attitudinal or emotional bank account for the AC4P Movement. S/he becomes more committed to the AC4P mission of building positive relations at his/her school and developing culture of interpersonal compassion.

How can the principle of consistency influence AC4P behaviors and attitudes of someone who receives a feedforward wristband? You know the answer, right? By accepting the wristband and putting it on, the individual performs behaviors that reflect a positive attitude toward the AC4P Movement. If this person later logs on to the AC4P website and reports his/her positive exchange with a teacher or SRO, more behavioral deposits are made to support consistent and positive self-talk, attitudes, and affect toward the AC4P Movement.

Plus, this individual might receive supportive feedback for the website posting, since stories posted on the AC4P website are forwarded to that individual's Facebook page. This social support can serve as more Feedforward to multiply AC4P behavior.

Eventually this continual spiraling of interpersonal feedforward fueling AC4P behavior supported by interpersonal supportive feedback can result in a genuine personal commitment to the AC4P Movement.

Discussion Questions

The instructor should facilitate interactive discussions of the following questions, perhaps in small groups and followed by reports to the entire audience.

1. What positive short-term and long-term consequences are likely if school personnel and students successfully spread the AC4P Movement throughout their school and beyond? Note how answers to this question can motivate individual and group execution of AC4P behavior (Lesson 1).

_____

_____

_____

_____

_____

_____

2. What is the value of recording each delivery and receipt of an AC4P wristband?

_____

_____

_____

_____

_____

_____

3. How can teachers and SROs be "motivated" to record their SAPS experiences at the AC4P Website?

_____

_____

_____

_____

_____

_____

4. What factors might hold back someone from initiating and maintaining the SAPS process? How can these potential barriers be minimized?

_____

_____

_____

_____

_____

_____

5. What kind of support could facilitate the large-term success of the AC4P Movement at your school?

_____

_____

_____

_____

_____

_____

6. Is there more to the AC4P Movement than the SAPS process? Please explain.

_____

_____

_____

_____

_____

_____

_____

7. What are the most important take-a-ways from this education/training program? What principles and/or procedures covered in this manual and discussed in your education/training program are most useful to you?

_____

_____

_____

_____

_____

_____

8. In what ways are the principles applied in the AC4P Movement useful beyond your job? How might you apply these principles or procedures in situations beyond your school?

_____

_____

_____

_____

_____

9. What did you like best about this education/training process?

_____

_____

_____

_____

_____

_____

10. How could this education/training for the AC4P Movement be improved?

_____

_____

_____

_____

_____

_____

ROLE PLAYING EXERCISE

This final role-playing exercise is most critical. Participants should practice the interpersonal communication steps of delivering an AC4P wristband as both feedforward and feedback, and explaining the SAPS process.

This can be accomplished by having participants pair off and play the role of "giver" and "receiver" of a feedforward and feedback delivery of an AC4P wristband. Later, volunteers could "replay" their interactions before the entire group of participants, followed by feedback from the instructor and other observers.

Or, participants can stay with their discussion groups and develop a role-play demonstration for the entire group. It would be enjoyable and perhaps instructive to create a role play of both wrong and right ways to deliver and receive an AC4P wristband as feedforward and feedback.

The purpose: to help participants feel comfortable giving people an AC4P wristband as feedforward and feedback, and explaining the SAPS process. As mentioned, achieving this level of comfort is challenging, but participation should be motivated by realizing the numerous positive consequences of promoting and supporting the AC4P Movement at your school.

IN CONCLUSION

Congratulations! You have just learned leading-edge principles and procedures for improving other people's behavior, while also increasing positive connections between you, your colleagues, and the students you serve.

I sincerely hope you have acquired more than an *understanding* of the seven principles of humanistic behaviorism (the academic term for the foundation of the AC4P Movement). I hope you *believe* in the validity of these research-based principles to improve interpersonal attitudes and behavior related to nourishing an AC4P culture.

Most important, I hope you feel *empowered* to begin practicing the principles with your family, colleagues, and eventually the students you serve at your school. Implementing the feedforward and feedback techniques with empathy will surely reap observable benefits. Plus, when you reflect on the results of your behavior-focused conversations, you continuously improve your skills at using one-to-one conversation to benefit the behavior of others.

When you add the AC4P wristband and the SAPS process to your communications with colleagues and students at your school, you maximize the positive consequences of each conversation. You will have recruited another participant for the AC4P Movement, and helped to nurture an AC4P culture of interpersonal trust, empathy, compassion, and routine acts of kindness.

The result: A school resource officer (SRO) will be viewed as a proactive agent of positive change rather than a negative law-enforcement official who only reacts to antisocial behavior or crises with punitive consequences. Similarly, teachers and other school personnel will be perceived as AC4P leaders. They tap the best in their students by inspiring self-motivation and an achievement-oriented mindset of continuous improvement.

SUGGESTED READINGS

Biglan, A. (2015). *The nurture effect: How the science of human behavior can improve our lives and our world*. Oakland, CA: New Harbinger Publications, Inc.

Geller, E.S. (2016) (Ed.). *Actively caring for people: Cultivating a culture of compassion* (5th Edition). Newport, VA: Make-A-Difference, LLC.

Geller, E.S. (2016) (Ed.). *Applied psychology: Actively caring for people*. New York: Cambridge University Press.

PERSONAL STORIES OF AC4P

Actively Caring is a get-well card sent to a friend, even a stranger; a cup of tea and a listening ear; returning found merchandise to its rightful owner; or shoveling a pile of snow from an elderly person's driveway. AC4P means we appreciate people for who they *are*, rather than what they've *achieved*. When stressors and life's conflicts take the heart out of us, we need to know someone cares about our difficulties and believes in us. And we need to reciprocate, and do the same for others.

AC4P makes a lasting difference in our lives. It's not about being judgmental, slashing people's self-esteem, and picking over faults. Not at all, AC4P values are uniqueness. It recognizes our human potential, and plays positively to our strengths.

Empathy is a prerequisite. We need to perceive and care about the concerns or predicaments of others. When called to act on our caring for others, we draw on our inner compassion and courage to act.

The following personal stories demonstrate principles and applications of AC4P. They will inspire you to carve out more time to actively care for your family, friends, colleagues, and even strangers. Each story illustrates how an AC4P mindset brings out the best in both the giver and the receiver.

These testimonies bring home an important point: AC4P behavior strengthens your compassion and caring—you are the person giving. Imagine the AC4P cascade effect when ever-increasing numbers of individuals experience the rewarding, positive and healthy consequences of actively caring for others.

Leaping to the self-transcendent state that sits atop Maslow's Hierarchy of Needs fulfills our lower-level needs, especially our need for self-esteem and belongingness. Self-efficacy, personal control, and optimism are also strengthened through AC4P behavior. Empowerment and self-motivation are fueled by each of these person-states, and vice versa.

Our greatest challenge is to help others truly feel the rewarding power of AC4P behavior. To do this, we must develop the context and implement contingencies to motivate initial stirrings of AC4P behavior. The positive consequences of the AC4P behavior witnessed and experienced time and again in the following personal stories support the premise that AC4P behavior can come naturally—it is organically rewarding and self-sustaining when nurtured within a supportive culture.

These personal stories are not due to the competence, commitment and courage of a single heroic person. Friends, family, teachers, co-workers, and even strangers provide direction, mentorship or supportive consequences. Each story illustrates how AC4P principles enable the development of an AC4P culture—a culture of compassion at school, at work, at home, and throughout our communities.

THE IMPACT OF THE AC4P WRISTBAND

My son's elementary school has a wonderful program where the children are able to submit in writing a kind act by another classmate. All submissions are evaluated on a daily basis and two children are selected to wear the wristband for an entire day. All of the teachers and children are aware of the significance of wearing an AC4P wristband.

Last week, my son, Jacob, assisted a child who was hurt on the playground by helping him get to the nurse's office. The injured child submitted Jacob's kind act, and on Friday, he became the proud recipient of the green "Actively Caring for

People" wristband for the day. At the conclusion of the school day, he couldn't wait to come home and tell me about what had happened; however, he forgot to return the wristband to his teacher and it came home with him.

Jacob has a younger sister and she was as proud of him as his dad and I were. Unfortunately, she was playing with the wristband and pulled it to see how far it would stretch, and it broke. Jacob was devastated. Although we have tried to super glue the wristband back together, he is distraught that the one item each child is trying very hard to earn the right to wear, is broken. What should we do?!

The AC4P team sent a replacement wristband to the classroom teacher, and the class continued on with the AC4P process. Jacob's story suggests this wristband represents more than a reward—it's an esteemed token of appreciation and a symbol of the students' shared vision to cultivate a more compassionate classroom.

A STUDENT'S NOTE TO THE PRINCIPAL

A gym teacher met with a student after he bullied another student. They discussed why it was wrong and the student owned up to his behavior, but his next gesture was a surprise. The student wrote a note to the Principal to apologize for his actions. The end of the note said, "I am sorry for what I did, it was not actively caring."

Some of us feel guilty when we don't live up to our AC4P mission. At times, we may use guilt and shame interchangeably, but these terms are distinctly different. After performing non-AC4P behavior (i.e., bullying), some might feel guilt: "My behavior was bad;" others feel shame: "I am a bad person". Prior research has shown children with higher scores on guilt also score higher on prosocial behavior.[30]

The student who apologized via a note to the Principal might recognize the discrepancy between his actual behavior (non-AC4P) and ideal behavior (AC4P). The student's response focused on his negative behavior being wrong (guilt), but not labeling himself a bad person (shame). This reflects the AC4P principle of targeting the behavior—not the person—when giving corrective feedback (Lesson 3).

The AC4P approach makes prosocial behavior an expectation for students. It facilitates guilt in a student who failed to live up to the school-wide expectations. When we perceive our behavior as contrary to our values or our ideal-self, we feel guilt or cognitive dissonance, and usually try to resolve this discrepancy by changing our behavior.[31]

A TRIP TO THE PUMPKIN PATCH

Most students' love practicing the AC4P process and recognizing each other's classroom behavior with a wristband. We've collected a variety of AC4P stories from and about students. Here's just one:

We took our elementary students on a field trip to the pumpkin patch a few days before Halloween. After some time, they noticed a college-age student working and spotted a wristband. One student had the courage to ask what words were on the green wristband. "Actively Caring for People," said the worker.

The students were in awe. At that moment, they realized AC4P is something that goes beyond themselves, beyond their school and into the community. AC4P is not just a program in schools, but a Movement spreading beyond Virginia Tech to a pumpkin patch and communities worldwide.

ALY NEEL'S METRO STORY

After living in D.C. for some time and riding the Metro during many rush-hour mornings and nights, I have become well aware of the unwritten rule, "You just ride."

On my way home from work one day, I catch the redline train toward Union Station per usual. A young man, wearing a suit, sits inches away from me. He's so close I can almost touch him. I look up and notice he seems very upset—wringing his hands, shaking his head. Unintentionally, I stare at him. I try but can't look away; he seems on the verge of tears.

I immediately think, "What can I do?" I know I have to say something, but I'm uncertain how to reach out. We finally make eye contact, and I give him a smile—the empathic kind I would give a friend whose family member just died. I want him to know I'm sorry for whatever he is going through. Immediately after our exchange I look down, sort of embarrassed. I remember people aren't *supposed* to smile at each other on the Metro!

The Metro slows down and comes to a stop. The guy, still shaken up, stands to get off the train, but then pauses to touch me on my shoulder. He says: "You probably already forgot what you did. It didn't seem like a big deal, but this year has been the worst year of my life. What you just did a second ago, though really small, is probably the most anyone has reached out to me in this past year."

Rolling up his shirtsleeve, he tells me, "It represents a pay-it-forward notion." He hands me a green wristband, embossed with the words "Actively Caring for People." My mouth is agape. I had heard of this AC4P Movement, but I had never received a wristband until now.

AC4P INTERNET STORIES

Stories posted at ac4p.org tell of exchanges between people receiving and giving AC4P wristbands after specific AC4P behaviors. Wristband recognition occurs for simple gestures—such as holding the door for a stranger—and more complex acts requiring skills, financial stability, and time. These acts occur in many locations, including schools, restaurants, highways, community streets, and stores.

Many stories reflect competence, commitment, and courage. They involve ordinary people acting for the benefit of family, friends, co-workers, and strangers in both reactive circumstances and in proactive situations.

Some individuals receive a wristband for AC4P behavior in reactive situations, such as standing up for a friend after hearing a racist remark (wristband #407); rebuilding a home after tornadoes devastated Joplin, Missouri (#4766); helping after a sibling's car broke down (#2974); and saving the life of a motorcyclist after a crash (#240).

Others are recognized for proactive AC4P behavior, such as helping a friend, holding the door for extended periods of time, walking an intoxicated stranger to her home safely, taking care of a sick roommate, and giving a wallet thick with money back to the stranger who lost it (an act of caring requiring a certain degree of personal financial stability).

FROM RANDOM TO INTENTIONAL KINDNESS

Every story is unique, involving different people, places, and behaviors. One thread runs through each act of kindness: Intention. You've heard of "Random Acts of Kindness."[32] It implies acts of kindness "just happen" without planning or forethought. But as discussed earlier, most compassionate acts of helping others don't "just happen".

Every AC4P act reminds us to be mindful and intentional (i.e., System 2 thinking[33]) of opportunities to actively care. AC4P stories suggest those who actively care receive a rewarding return on their investment: smiles from strangers and genuine appreciation from friends. They think to themselves, "That could've been worse if I hadn't actively cared," or "I really made my friend's day."

I hope these stories inspire you to recognize others with AC4P wristbands whenever you see intentional acts of caring. Such AC4P behavior ranges from small acts of kindness to heroic demonstrations of courage. Your AC4P servant leadership helps cultivate a culture of compassion worldwide.

The following AC4P stories were selected from more than 5,000 posted on the ac4p.org website since January 2011. The stories depict instances of individuals extending themselves beyond what society expects, stepping up and intervening as a concerned and compassionate bystander for the health, safety, and/or well-being of someone else.

FROM AN AC4P WRISTBAND TO AN AC4P LIFESTYLE

My freshman year I was lucky to have some crazy roommates who truly tested everything about me. At this point, I was a rough and temperamental` personality trying to fit my way into the world, but struggling to adapt. However, I was given something from Benjamin Caleb George. It was a green wristband with the following words inscribed: "Actively Caring for People." At first, I wore the wristband to make Ben happy (sorry Ben but hey it's true), but the words started to etch their way into my life. I found myself trying to become better for everyone, including my friends.

It was tough and I can be a dramatic handful at times, but my life became better and I found myself smiling every day. Today, I lost that green wristband—the one that has been with me for two years, showing up in every good and bad photo. I didn't notice until I looked down and it was gone.

Its weight and words truly have sunk into my skin and I guess it has done its job. So I want to thank Ben for giving me something he might not even know would have a huge effect on my life. And for everyone who has been by my side this whole time, I know it isn't easy and you didn't have to be there, but you were. For that, I thank you. I still have more work to do to better myself, but at least I have a great start.

Nathaniel C.
Richmond, VA

A COMPASSIONATE TRUCK DRIVER

I am currently on my way back home to Virginia from New York. Long story short, my car broke down. Stuck on the side of the road we called AAA. A tow truck came, with a driver by the name of Taka (Take-a). This man is trying everything in his power to get us all the way from Middletown, Delaware to Virginia Beach, Virginia (some 215 miles) without charging us $500 dollars. He is sticking his neck out to do something for two stranded women that wouldn't benefit him at all. True human compassion! *Wristband #2974*

Jenee E.

Middletown, DE

OFFERING A SEAT

Today, I was in Au Bon Pain and saw two girls offer a seat at their table to a blind student during the busy lunch hour. Then, they proceeded to put down their homework and have a conversation with her, as well as refill her drink when it was empty.

Without acts of kindness like these, I don't know if the student would have ever found a table during the rush hour at Au Bon Pain! I was so ecstatic to be able to give out my first wristband, especially to somebody who truly went out of her way to make somebody else's day! *Wristband #168*

Elise C.

Blacksburg, VA

COMING TO THE RESCUE

My car has had a lot go wrong with it in the past year or so. I never take care of it. The "Check Engine" and "Maint Required" lights have been on for as long as I can remember, and it's been a joke that any day now the thing might explode (not really, I hope).

I let my boyfriend borrow my car one day, and when he returned it my brake light was fixed, the "Check Engine" and "Maint Required" lights were off, there was a brand new cap on my gas tank (I had lost it before), my oil had been checked, and fluid had been put in my windshield wiper thing.

Turns out my boyfriend had taken my car in to get a full list of what was wrong with it (a long list) and wanted to fix everything. But he doesn't know a lot about cars. Turns out Dave came to the rescue! Dave is my boyfriend's roommate. He happens to know a lot about cars and took the extra time to look over and fix the long list of things wrong with it, just because! *Wristband #22549*

Michelle L.

Blacksburg, VA

HELPING A MISSING CHILD

I was at Great Wolf lodge when the front desk called to ask if I was missing a child. I said, "No." When I woke up the next morning, I saw a lady with the missing boy.

The missing child had been in the lobby all night with the lady. She got him blankets and held him. I learned she'd been there for seven hours taking care of that boy. The boy's dad didn't even know when he woke up that his son was gone. I gave my wristband to "the lady of the night," someone who actively cared! *Wristband #1425*

Logan O.

Charlotte, NC

A COMPASSIONATE STUDENT PATROL

A student member of the safety patrol, Eli, showed compassion to another student who boarded my bus in tears. The student proceeded to fight with her older siblings; one of them being Eli's peer.

Eli handled the situation beyond what is required of the safety patrol. She was able to immediately calm the child and find a resolution to what would have surely escalated into something very distracting for me as the bus driver. It allowed me to carry on instead of waiting for a safe place to pullover to address the situation myself. I gave him *Wristband #8215*

Jennifer S.

Great Falls, VA

A VERY GRATEFUL STUDENT AND FELLOW HOKIE

I don't usually post stories but I thought this one was an awesome testament to the kind of people we have in Blacksburg. I am driving down Southgate toward Airport Drive and hit something in the middle of the road. My tire immediately bursts and I have to pull over. Of course I have no idea what to do. I get out and call my parents, as if they can help from four hours away.

With no answer, I'm scared and unsure what to do. The first few cars fly by me and then finally an older gentleman offers to help. He immediately starts changing the tire and asks me to simply direct traffic. As I'm standing in the middle of the four-way intersection a student walks by. He drops his book bag and rushes over to help me.

After a few minutes of feeling like I'm going to be hit in the middle of the intersection, I call the Blacksburg Police Department to take over. In a matter of minutes two officers respond and thank me for doing the best I could. I have the spare tire in place, the student begins describing the "Actively Caring" campaign and he gives the older gentleman one of the green wristbands we have all seen around campus.

Until now I didn't know what "paying it forward" really meant. My crazy day turned out to be a story I'll never forget and one I will tell a million times to show people what it really means to be a Hokie. I wouldn't trade this school and town for anything in the world. UT PROSIM, and GO HOKIES. *Wristband #2517*

Kelley C.
Blacksburg, VA

BYSTANDER INTERVENTION STORIES

AC4P BEHAVIOR SAVES A LIFE

I witnessed a man wreck a dirt bike crashing through a glass window. Once I heard the breaking glass, I ran to the scene and saw lacerations on his arm and several on his leg. I knew this was serious when I saw the amount of blood he lost in the 20 or so seconds it took for me to get there.

I, along with another Appalachian State University student, used t-shirts to stop the bleeding and make him comfortable until the paramedics arrived. He received more than 200 stitches for all of his wounds. We were told he would have bled out if his bleeding had not been stopped right away. Wristband #240

Riley S.

Boone, NC

CORRECTIVE FEEDBACK FOR A RACIST REMARK

I invited my friend to hang out at our fraternity house. You might not know right away by looking at him, but he has a white mother and a black father. For most members of the fraternity, this is not an issue.

However, when we were on the porch one of the brothers, unknowing of my friend's ethnicity, begins yelling racist remarks. I immediately confronted my bro in front of guests and other brothers and told him to stop, that his bigotry was unacceptable.

After the fact, I felt guilty to belong to an organization where this kind of racism was present, and I felt incredibly troubled that my guest experienced this at my house. I didn't know the impact of standing up for my friend until he presented me with this green wristband. The next chapter meeting we established a rule and judiciary system to handle out-of-line hostile or harassing behavior. Wristband #10805

Scott M.
Statesboro, GA

STOPPING TO HELP ON I-95

It was the day after Christmas on a Sunday morning at 6 A.M. I'm a nurse and was driving into Baltimore for work.

I was cruising on I-95 just like every morning and saw a car that appeared stalled in the middle of the interstate about 100 feet ahead. I pulled into the right lane and slowed down. As I approached, I realized this car in the middle of the road was totaled and none of its lights were on. I immediately pulled onto the side of the road and reached into my pocket to pull out my phone to dial 911.

Before I was able to call, a woman squeezed out of the wrecked car and came running to the side of the road where I was, holding her chest. I got out of my car and asked what had happened. She told me her car was hit by another car, causing her to spin, and then a tractor-trailer slammed into her vehicle. Both the other car and tractor-trailer drove off, leaving her car smashed in the middle of the road.

I got on the phone with the police while helping to keep her calm and assessing her to make sure she was alright. As this was going on, cars were weaving around her car, which was still in the middle of the road. All of a sudden an SUV crashes into her car, causing it to go flying to the side of the road about 30 feet from where we were standing. That's when I really realized: This situation is extremely dangerous.

The SUV driver got out and came running to where we were. I helped keep both of them calm, got their medical history, and assessed them for injuries—all before the police and an ambulance finally arrived. As the woman was being loaded into the ambulance, I noticed she too was wearing scrubs and was a nurse on her way to work, just like me.

I just told my brother this story today and when I did, he pulled off his wristband and gave it to me, telling me to tell my story and pass on the wristband. So that's what I will do. *Wristband #17630*

Alicia C.
Baltimore, MD

HELPING A STRANGER ON THE SIDE OF THE ROAD

The other day my car battery died and left me stranded. When I finally got a hold of my mom, she came and tried to jump my battery, which unfortunately fried her car's battery too, leaving us both in a rut.

While my mom started her trek to her nearest friend's house, I waited by our cars. After about 20 minutes of watching cars whiz by, a student from a neighboring district pulled over and asked if I needed any help. Not only did he stay with me as it started to get dark, but he also called his dad who happened to be an auto mechanic. His dad selflessly came and fixed both my mother's and my own car.

I gave my wristband for actively caring to the boy for being the one out of the majority who pulled over to help me—a complete stranger. *Wristband #38955*

Abi C.
Chagrin Falls, OH

CARING FOR VICTIMS OF A CAR CRASH

I arrived on the scene of a head-on car crash that happened directly in front of us. I and several friends got out to help. I went to one of the cars that had some serious damage and found a young girl inside. Both drivers' side doors were jammed shut.

When I went around to the passenger side I discovered her legs were pinned between the seat and steering wheel/dashboard. While another passerby dialed 911, I got her to give me her parents' phone number. I called them to let them know what was going on.

I stayed with her and tried to keep her calm until the paramedics arrived. Later, after some time went by, she got my number from her parents and called. She said she had a wristband to give me and wanted my address. A short time later I got the wristband in the mail. *Wristband #12548*

Joey B.
Chesterfield, VA

COMPASSION DURING TIMES OF HARDSHIP

My sister's husband recently passed away after an extended illness. As she finished the difficult task of going through his closet, she wondered what do to with his nearly new (and even some brand new) business and casual clothes. She saw the bus driver for the faith-based school where she teaches and noticed he always wears t-shirts and jeans. She was aware this was because of financial hardship and not a fashion statement. She asked his size and it was the same as her husband's new clothes.

She gave him all of the clothes that fit him—outfitting him with an entirely new wardrobe. He and his family are so grateful. I've sent the wristband to my sister and I know she'll not only pass it on—but continue (as she has) to actively care for people. She is an inspiration to me and all of our family. *Wristband #15260*

Theresa S.
Taylor, TX

STRENGTHENING FRIENDSHIP

I recently passed a wristband on to one of my friends at Summer Residential Governor's School. A girl I know was giving me a hard time while a bunch of our friends were spending time together. I left the room, clearly upset, to spend the rest of the night in my dorm rather than provoking the girl even more. My friend, agreeing the girl's comments were out of line, came up to spend the rest of the night in my dorm room with me. We talked mostly about other things.

I thought it was incredibly sweet of my friend to go out of her way to cheer me up. By giving her the wristband I let her know she means a lot to me as a friend and I really appreciate her. She got a little teary-eyed (in happiness of course).

My first experience giving someone an AC4P wristband was one I will truly never forget because I grew much closer to a friend as a result. :] *Wristband #12576*

Melissa D.
Radford, VA

WHAT GOES AROUND COMES AROUND

I have always been a proponent of *pay it forward* and when I initially heard of AC4P, I 1felt like a younger generation now had to chance to pay it forward and understand the benefits.

My story began last winter at a restaurant. I saw a family who was told by the hostess to stand outside in the cold. I quickly finished my dinner and asked that they be seated at our table. The family was from out of town, visiting their daughter, and was truly appreciative.

Fast forward to this summer. My youngest daughter and I were at a local supermarket. I had forgotten my wallet, but we had checks. However, since I did not have my license, the clerk told me to put my groceries back. Out from behind the line, a young female said, "I will pay for her." I thanked her and tried to write her a check, but she would not take it.

Then, a different young female came from the door and ran up to the girl who paid for me. She said, "You are actively caring, here's a wristband for you, pass it on." I screamed with joy and my seven-year-old child smiled.

After leaving, I realized the girl who paid for me in the grocery store was Catherine—the same young girl to whom I gave my seat at the restaurant six months earlier. Pay it forward! Actively Caring for People can become a global Movement with your help!

Donna Wertalik
Blacksburg, VA

FROM ONE AC4P ACT TO ANOTHER

A few weeks ago, Dr Geller came through the door, buzzing with excitement. He had just been to his bank and Dalton, one of the bank tellers, told him she had a story she needed to share.

She had been at Panera Bread, venting on her cell-phone about an unpleasant event. Frustrated, Dalton hung up, after saying, "I'm in Panera now, I'll call you later."

After she ordered, the man behind the counter smiled and told her he'd pay for her meal because she was having a bad day. Grateful, and her day brightened, Dalton prepared to pass on the wristband she'd received weeks before only to realize she had forgotten it at home.

She explained this to him, saying she wanted to pass him the AC4P wristband. Mat proudly displayed his wrist, revealing a green AC4P wristband, "It's alright, I already have one." He had received *Wristband #5707* two weeks earlier from Joanne Dean Geller.

Eric Cunningham & Ilana Elias
NSF & MAOP Students
Blacksburg, VA

ACKNOWLEDGEMENTS

For more than 35 years, I've taught AC4P principles and applications in workshops and keynotes at regional and national conferences, as well at various Fortune 500 Companies. The evidence-based AC4P lessons have always been well-received. However, periodically my evaluations have included a critical comment such as, "I appreciate the theory and principles presented by Dr. Geller, but I don't know how to apply his teachings. I like the ideas, but he didn't tell me what to do with them."

This education/training manual addressed this legitimate concern in the best way possible. How? By combining seven research-based principles of humanistic behaviorism with instructions for practical tried-and-true applications, designed to cultivate a positive and cooperative educational culture that optimizes both teaching and learning.

After a principle was explained with definitions, examples, and illustrations, questions were asked the reader and practice exercises were recommended to activate customization of the evidence-based principles for specific solutions relevant for the reader or workshop participants. Thus, I've written this handbook for more than reading. Rather, it's for learning, practicing, refining, and owning the humanistic behaviorism lessons for use throughout the school day, and then at home with friends and family.

The vision of a book to teach AC4P principles and applications could not have become a reality without the support of several key individuals, beginning with Bobby Kipper, the author of the inspirational Foreword and the Director of the National Center for Prevention of Community Violence (NCPCV, www. solveviolence.com).

Profound knowledge relevant to the improvement of human welfare is useless without change agents (e.g., teachers, consultants, community leaders, work supervisors, and parents) willing and capable to take this knowledge to potential users in a form that is accepted and appreciated by those individuals. Bobby Kipper and his staff at the NCPCV are exemplary agents of large-scale beneficial change—informing, activating, and supporting the public regarding the real-world applications of research-based principles relevant for improving quality of life, especially interventions that prevent interpersonal conflict and encourage acts of kindness throughout a community.

Bobby and the NCPCV embraced the principles and applications of humanistic behaviorism immediately, and have been disseminating these in communities nationwide, especially in schools and police departments. Indeed, it has been less than two years since Bobby and I first met, and since that time his organization has: 1) sponsored a retreat to take AC4P principles to leaders of police departments, an event that was covered by Fox News (www.foxnews. com),[34] 2) worked with me on the development of a training manual on AC4P Policing, supported by an NCPCV website (www.ac4ppolicing.org) and blue AC4P wristbands,[35] 3) initiated the development of an online course on AC4P Policing, soon to be disseminated nationwide, 4) delivered several keynote addresses and workshops on AC4P for police officers and SROs, 5) organized an anti-bullying conference at Virginia Tech and a follow-up retreat at Make-A-Diff Ranch in Newport, VA, and 6) inspired me to prepare this guidebook, knowing the NCPCV will contribute significantly to getting this scholarship in the hands of school personnel and SROs who can put the AC4P principles to good use.

I also want to acknowledge the education/training and consultancy of Safety Performance Solutions, Inc. (www.safteyperformance.com)—its team of partners, my collaborators, who have been teaching the AC4P principles and applications covered in this manual to organizations worldwide since 1994. Thus, this organization has verified the social validity of the contents of this manual by using the principles to reduce the injury rates of numerous companies worldwide for more than two decades.

Thirdly, I am indebted to the long-term advice, alliance, and friendship of Dave Johnson, editor of *Industrial Safety & Hygiene News* (*ISHN*). Dave and I began collaborating in 1990 when I submitted my first five articles for publication in his magazine. Every time one of my articles was published, I learned something about communicating more effectively a principle or practice from humanistic behaviorism. This invaluable learning experience continued for the 19 consecutive years of my monthly *ISHN* column: *The Psychology of Safety.*

Dave was the editor of my first safety book—*The Psychology of Safety* [36] and two subsequent textbooks on people-based safety [37], and our recent textbook on *Applied Psychology* [38]. Plus, we co-authored a volume that teaches the relevant humanistic behaviorism to healthcare works—*People-Based Patient Safety: Enriching your culture to prevent medical error.* [39]

In all of our collaborations, including this teaching/learning handbook, Dave added his "magic" to the written expression and made it more concise, clear, and reader-friendly. His coaching helped me make my scholarship more accessible and appreciated by the general public. Indeed, if the contents of this book are not understood and embraced by masses of people beyond the ivory tower of my University, the evidence-based principles and procedural recommendations reported here have no chance of making the beneficial culture difference they were designed to make.

What about the creative, instructive and entertaining illustrations interspersed throughout this manual? Since 1990, my teaching, textbooks, and workbooks have benefitted from the artistic talents of George Wills of Blacksburg, VA.

Plus, I am very grateful for the dedication of my Virginia Tech students and associates in our University Center for Applied Behavior Systems (CABS) who collect and analyze endless streams of field data to test the impact of various AC4P interventions, and inform the design of more effective procedures to increase the frequency and improve the quality of AC4P behavior.

The support system of CABS serves as a "think tank" for considering innovative approaches to understanding and influencing the human dynamics of interpersonal compassion and for developing research procedures to analyze variables that could affect the success of the AC4P Movement. In this regard, I am particularly beholden to my current graduate students: Devin Carter, Nick Flannery, Trevin Glasgow, Micah Roediger, and Bryce Torian, as well as our current CABS Coordinators: Brian Doyle and Ashley Underwood.

Ashley word-processed and formatted the entire contents of this book, including the painstaking deciphering of my handwritten text and continuous improvement editing.

Last but certainly not least, I am appreciative of the competent support of the staff at Morgan James Publishers, beginning with the vision of David Hancock, who saw the potential of a practical teaching/learning manual to teach the AC4P principles and applications to police officers, school personnel, and SROs. Then we were privileged to have the support of Margo Toulouse's team at Morgan James who designed the cover, and formatted the scholarship for publication.

My 47-year teaching and research career at Virginia Tech, reflected by much of the contents in this education/training manual, has benefitted hugely from an extensive support system in both the academic and consulting worlds—professional colleagues, university students, and consumers of my books and education/training programs. All of you have offered constructive feedback to help me improve, and you've inspired me to keep on keeping on.

Thank you all very much. The synergy from your past, present, and future sustenance enables a legacy—AC4P principles and practices readers can use to enrich their lives and contribute to cultivating cultures of interpersonal compassion at school, at home, and in every environment where humanistic behaviorism can make a beneficial difference.

E. Scott Geller

NOTES

1. Colvin, G., Tobin, T., Beard, K., Hagan, S., & Sprague, J. (1998). The school bully: Assessing the problem, developing interventions, and future research directions. *Journal of Behavioral Education, 8*(3), 293-319.
2. Ttofi, M.M., & Farrington, D.P. (2010). Effectiveness of school-based programs to reduce bullying: A systematic and meta-analytical review. *Journal of Experimental Criminology, 7*(1), 27-56.
3. Swearer, S.M., Espelage, D.L., Vaillancourt, T., & Hymel, S. (2010). What can be done about school bullying? Linking research to educational practice. *Educational Researcher, 39*, 38-47.
4. Sidman, M. (1989). *Coercion and its fallout.* Boston, MA: Authors Cooperative.
5. Roland, E. (2002). Aggression, depression, and bullying others. *Aggressive Behavior, 28*, 198-206.
6. Miltenberger, R.G. (1997). *Behavior modification: Principles and procedures.* Pacific Grove, CA: Brooks-Cole; Ogier, R., & Hornby, G. (1996). Effects of differential reinforcement on the behavior and self-esteem of children with emotional and behavioral disorders. *Journal of Behavioral Education, 6*(4), 501-510.
7. Simpson, B., & Willer, R. (2008). Altruism and indirect reciprocity: The interaction of person and situation in prosocial behavior. *Social Psychology Quarterly, 71*(1), 37-52.

8. Honig, A.S., & Pollack, B. (1990). Effects of a brief intervention program to promote prosocial behaviors in young children. *Early Education and Development, 1*(6), 438–444.

9. Demaray, M.K., & Malecki, C.K. (2006). A review of the use of social support in anti-bullying programs. *The Journal of School Violence, 5*(3), 51-70.

10. Whitted, S., & Dupper, R.D. (2005). Best practices for preventing or reducing bullying in schools. *Children &School, 27*(3), 167-175.

11. Geller, E.S. (2001). *The psychology of safety handbook.* Boca Raton, FL: CRC Press.

12. Wentzel, K.R., Barry, C.M., & Caldwell, K.A. (2004). Friendships in middle school: Influences on motivation and school adjustment. *Journal of Educational Psychology, 96*(2), 195-203.

13. Hoglund, W., & Leadbeater, B. (2004). The effects of family, school, and classroom ecologies on changes in children's social competence and emotional and behavioral problems in first grade. *Developmental Psychology, 40*(4), 533-544.

14. Feldman, R.S., Philippot, P., & Custrini, R.J. (1991). In R.S. Feldman & B. Rime (Eds.). *Fundamentals of nonverbal behavior* (pp. 329-350). Cambridge, MA: Cambridge University Press.

15. Cook, C.R., Williams, K.R., Guerra, N.G., Kim, T.E., & Sadek, S. (2010). Predictors of bullying and victimization in childhood and adolescence: A meta-analytical investigation. *School Psychology Quarterly, 25*(2), 65-83.

16. McCarty, S.M., & Geller, E.S. (2011). Want to get rid of bullying? Then reward behavior that is incompatible with it. *Behavior Analysis Digest International, 23*(2), 1-7; McCarty, S.M., Teie, S., McCutchen, J., & Geller, E.S. (2016). Actively caring to prevent bullying in an elementary school: Prompting and rewarding prosocial behavior. *Journal of Prevention & Intervention in the Community, 44*(3), 164-176.

17. Raboteau, A. (2011, July 25). Psychology professor, students say recognizing daily acts of kindness makes a huge impact. *Virginia Tech: Spotlight*. Retrieved from http://www.vt.edu/spotlight/impact/2011-07-25-caring/movement.html\

18. Geller, E.S. (2016) (Ed). *Actively caring for people: Cultivating a culture of compassion* (5th Edition). Newport VA: Make-A-Difference, LLC; Geller, E.S. (2016) (Ed). *Applied psychology: Actively caring for people.* New York: Cambridge University Press; Geller, E.S. (2016). Seven life lessons from humanistic behaviorism: How to bring the best out of yourself and others. *Journal of Organizational Behavior Management, 35*(1), 151-170.

19. Carnegie, D. (1936). *How to win friends and influence people* (1981Edition). New York: Simon and Schuster, p. 19.

20. Bandura, A. (1969). *Principles of behavior modification.* New York: Holt, Reinhold & Winston.

21. Dweck, C.S. (2006). *Mindset: The new psychology of success.* New York: Ballantine Books.

22. Chance, P. (2008). *The teacher's craft: The 10 essential skills of effective teaching.* Long Grove, IL: Waveland Press, Inc.; Reed, D. et al. (2016). Actively caring for higher education. In E.S. Geller (Ed.). *Applied psychology: Actively caring for people* (pp.563-593). New York: Cambridge University Press.

23. Thorndike, E.L. (1931). *Human learning.* Cambridge, MA: MIT Press.

24. Geller, E. S. (2001). *The psychology of safety handbook* (Chapter 15). Boca Raton, FL: CRC Press; Geller E.S. (2016). The psychology of AC4P behavior. In Geller, E.S. (Ed.). *Applied psychology: Actively caring for people* (pp. 45-82). New York: Cambridge University Press

25. Carnegie, D. (1936). *How to win friends and influence people* (1981 Edition). New York: Simon and Schuster

26. Covey, S.R. (1989). *The seven habits of highly effective people.* New York: Simon and Schuster.

27. Deci, E.L., & Flaste, R. (1995). *Why we do what we do: Understanding self-motivation.* New York: Penguin Books; Geller, E.S. (2016). The psychology of self-motivation. In Geller, E.S. (Ed.). *Applied psychology: Actively caring for people* (pp.83-118). New York: Cambridge University Press; Geller, E.S., & Veazie, R.A. (2010). *When no one's watching: Living and leading self-motivation.* Newport, VA: Make-A-Difference, LLC.

28. Maslow, A.H. (1971). *The farther reaches of human nature.* New York: Viking.

29. Cialdini, R.B. (2001). *Influence: Science and practice* (6th Edition). Boston, MA: Pearson Education; Furrow, C., & Geller, E.S. (2016). Social influence and AC4P behavior. In E.S. Geller (Ed.). *Applied psychology: Actively caring for people* (pp. 185-227). New York: Cambridge University Press.

30. Krevans, J., & Gibbs, J.C. (2008). Parents' use of inductive discipline: Relations to children's empathy and prosocial behavior. *Child Development,* 67(6), 3263-3277.

31. Festinger, L. (1957). *A theory of cognitive dissonance.* Stanford, CA: Stanford University Press.

32. Conari Press (1993). *Random acts of kindness.* Emeryville, CA.

33. Kahneman, D. (2011). *Thinking fast and slow.* New York: Farrar, Straus and Giroux.

34. Geller, E.S., & Kipper, B. (2015). AC4P Policing: A research-based process for cultivating positive police-community relations. *Police Chief,* September, p.41.

35. Geller, E.S., & Kipper, B. (2017). *Actively caring for people policing: Building positive police/citizen relations.* New York: Morgan James Publishers.

36. Geller, E. S. (1996). *The psychology of safety: How to improve behaviors and attitudes on the job.* Radnor, PA: Chilton Book Company.

37. Geller, E. S. (2005). *People-based safety: The source.* Virginia Beach, VA: Coastal Training and Technologies Corporation; Geller, E.S. (2008). *Leading people-based safety: Enriching your culture.* Virginia Beach, VA: Coastal Training and Technologies Corporation.
38. Geller, E.S. (2016) (Ed.). *Applied Psychology: Actively caring for people.* New York: Cambridge University Press.
39. Geller, E.S., & Johnson, D. (2008). *People-based patient safety: Enriching your culture to prevent medical error.* Virginia Beach, VA: Coastal Training and Technologies Corporation.

ABOUT THE AUTHOR

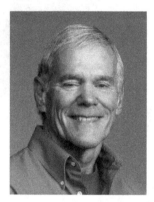 **E. Scott Geller**, Ph.D. is an Alumni Distinguished Professor in the Department of Psychology at Virginia Tech. For more than four decades, Professor Geller has taught and conducted research as a faculty member and director of the Center for Applied Behavior Systems in the Department of Psychology. He has authored, edited or co-authored 27 books, 82 book chapters, 39 training programs, 259 magazine articles, and more than 300 research articles addressing the development and evaluation of behavior-change interventions to improve quality of life on a large scale. His most recent book: *Applied Psychology: Actively Caring for People* defines Dr. Geller's research, teaching, and scholarship career at Virginia Tech, which epitomizes the VT logo: *Ut Prosim*—"That I May Serve".

His popular books in applied psychology include: *The Psychology of Safety: Improving behaviors and attitudes on the job*; *Working Safe*; *Understanding Behavior-Based Safety*; *Building Successful Safety Teams*; *Beyond Safety Accountability: How to increase personal responsibility*; *The Psychology of Safety Handbook*; *Keys to Behavior-Based Safety from Safety Performance Solutions*; *The Participation Factor*; *People-Based Safety: The Source*; *People-Based Patient Safety: Enriching your culture to prevent medical error*, coauthored by Dave Johnson. *Leading People-Based*

Safety: Enriching your culture; Actively Caring for People: Cultivating a culture of compassion; and *Actively Caring at Your School: How to make it happen; The Courage Factor: Leading people-based people change,* and *When No One's Watching: Living and leading self-motivation,* both coauthored by Bob Veazie, and *Actively caring for people policing: Building positive police/citizen relations,* coauthored by Bobby Kipper.

Dr. Geller is a Fellow of the American Psychological Society, the Association for Psychological Science, the Association of Behavior Analysis International, and the World Academy of Productivity and Quality Sciences. He is past Editor of the *Journal of Applied Behavior Analysis* (1989-1992), current Associate Editor of *Environment and Behavior* (since 1982), and current Consulting Editor for *Behavior and Social Issues,* the *Journal of Organizational Behavior Management,* and the *Journal of Safety Research.*

Dr. Geller has written more than 200 articles for *Industrial Safety and Hygiene News,* a trade magazine disseminated to more than 75,000 companies. He collaborated with Tel-A-Train Inc., J.J. Keller and Associates, and Coastal Training Technologies Corporation to develop various training series, which include videotapes or DVDs, workbooks, and facilitators' guides. For these innovative and creative works, beginning with a 1995 nationally renowned seminar series—Actively Caring for Safety—the Society for the Advancement of Behavior Analysis honored Dr. Geller with an award for Effective Presentation of Behavior Analysis in the Mass Media.

Scott Geller's dedication, talent, and energy have helped him earn a teaching award in 1982 from the American Psychological Association and every university-wide teaching award offered at Virginia Tech. Moreover, in 2001 Virginia Tech awarded Dr. Geller the University Alumni Award for Excellence in Research. In 2002, the University honored him with the Alumni Outreach Award for his exemplary real-world applications of behavioral science, and in 2003 he received the University Alumni Award for Graduate Student Advising. In 2005, he was awarded the statewide Virginia Outstanding Faculty Award by the State Council of Higher Education, and Virginia Tech conferred the title of Alumni Distinguished Professor on him.

Professor Geller has received lifetime achievement awards from the International Organizational Behavior Management Network (in 2008) and the American Psychological Foundation (in 2009). And in 2010 he was honored with the Outstanding Applied Research Award from the American Psychological Association's Division of Applied Behavior Analysis. In 2011, the College of Wooster awarded E. Scott Geller the honorary degree: Doctor of Humane Letters.

A free eBook edition is available with the purchase of this book.

To claim your free eBook edition:

1. Download the Shelfie app.
2. Write your name in upper case in the box.
3. Use the Shelfie app to submit a photo.
4. Download your eBook to any device.

Shelfie

A **free** eBook edition is available
with the purchase of this print book.

CLEARLY PRINT YOUR NAME ABOVE IN UPPER CASE

Instructions to claim your free eBook edition:
1. Download the Shelfie app for Android or iOS
2. Write your name in **UPPER CASE** above
3. Use the Shelfie app to submit a photo
4. Download your eBook to any device

Print & Digital Together Forever.

Snap a photo   Free eBook   Read anywhere

We connect Morgan James published authors with live and online events and audiences whom will benefit from their expertise.

9 781683 502494